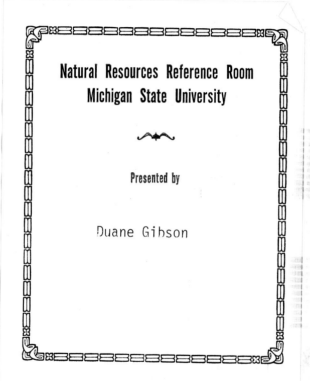

COMMUNITIES AND THEIR
DEVELOPMENT

Other books by the same author

Training for Community Development
School and Community in the Tropics
Problems of African Development
The Human Factor in Community Work

COMMUNITIES AND THEIR DEVELOPMENT

An Introductory Study with
Special Reference to the Tropics

T. R. BATTEN

*(Reader in Community Development Studies
University of London Institute of Education)*

LONDON
OXFORD UNIVERSITY PRESS

Oxford University Press, Amen House, London E.C.4

GLASGOW NEW YORK TORONTO MELBOURNE WELLINGTON
BOMBAY CALCUTTA MADRAS KARACHI LAHORE DACCA
CAPE TOWN SALISBURY NAIROBI IBADAN
KUALA LUMPUR HONG KONG

First edition 1957
Second impression 1960
Third impression 1962
Fourth impression 1964
Fifth impression 1965

REPRINTED BY LITHOGRAPHY IN GREAT BRITAIN
BY JARROLD AND SONS LIMITED, NORWICH

PREFACE

THE past ten years or so have seen a very rapid expansion of community development work, and nearly everywhere governments and voluntary agencies have been trying out new forms of organization, new methods and new techniques. In this book I aim to study some of these experiments and draw conclusions from them, bringing together information and ideas from many sources which are not all easily accessible to most workers in the tropics.

My main purpose is to study and compare differences in aim, method, and organization, and to illustrate each point with one or more examples. I have not tried to describe policies and methods country by country, and the fact that some countries are but sketchily represented and others, perhaps, not mentioned at all, is not intended to imply that they are not important. It means only that their ideas and methods are well enough illustrated by one or more of the examples actually selected. While all the chosen examples are necessarily local and particular, I hope that the conclusions drawn from them will be of interest and use to organizers and field workers everywhere.

Accurate, detailed knowledge of what is being attempted in many countries is difficult for the outsider to come by, yet on it must depend the validity of the conclusions reached and the usefulness of the book. I am aware of this difficulty and have done my best to overcome it. I have been greatly helped by experience in dealing with problems of community education while serving in West and East Africa from 1927 to 1949, and since 1949 by the work I have been doing at the University of London Institute of Education. There I have been making comparative studies of community development work with special reference to the tropics. This has meant making a systematic study of a wide range of reports, journals, and other publications, but even more important as sources of information have been sustained discussions with a large number of experienced serving officers ranging in seniority from assistant field officers to directors and deputy directors of development departments. About twenty such officers, men and women, come to the Institute each year to study community development or the techniques of extension work. Almost everything in this book has been hammered out in discussion with groups of these officers, and most of the examples have been checked for accuracy with one or more officers with a first-hand knowledge of the area or project concerned. In fact, many of the examples selected have been preferred to other examples just because it has been possible to check them in this way. Thus in a very real sense this book is a product of group study. Some 150 officers from more than thirty tropical and sub-tropical countries have in one way or another contributed to the ideas it contains.

I have been glad to have the opportunity provided by this fifth impression of revising and bringing up to date the list of books suggested for further reading on pp. 242-4.

T. R. BATTEN

University of London
Institute of Education,
    1965

CONTENTS

PLATES

CHAPTER I

INTRODUCTION

I T is difficult to state briefly, yet adequately, what community development is. There is no precise and generally accepted definition. Many people would agree with the authors of a recent community development report[1] in defining it as a process during which people in the small community first thoroughly discuss and define their wants, and then plan and act together to satisfy them. Here the stress is all on the community. Others, however, would stress the development agency's role. Thus at Cambridge, England, in 1948, it was defined at a conference of colonial administrators as

A movement to promote better living for the whole community, with the active participation and if possible on the initiative of the community, but if this initiative is not forthcoming, by the use of technique for arousing and stimulating it in order to secure its active and enthusiastic response to the movement. . . . *It includes the whole range of development activities in the districts, whether these are undertaken by government or unofficial bodies.*[1] (My italics.)

Here there is distinctly less emphasis on the community project. Community development is identified with almost any form of local betterment which is in some way achieved with the willing co-operation of the people.

Again, if we study the actual work that goes on in the field, we find we need an even wider definition. Some agencies hardly stress initiative at all. They plan specific, detailed programmes which they work to carry out. Others aim mainly to get communities themselves to think and plan and act. For them the way the people set about their work is more important than the work itself. They stress the process of community development rather than the product.

There are other differences, too. Some agencies lay more stress on education than on projects. Some work with the whole community, while others, e.g. the churches, may concentrate on smaller groups within it. Some stress the need for strengthening community, while others stress the need for enlarging individual freedom.

I am not writing to support some of these views and to condemn others, for all are valid and related to community development, but this does not mean that they all equally apply to every situation and to every community. Different communities have different needs, and the same community has different needs at different times. It is to finding and meeting these needs that agency aims and methods should be related, and it is by success in doing so, rather than by adhering to any fixed principles or dogma, that community agencies must justify what they do. The final authority for what the agency does is the 'authority' of the actual situation which confronts it. In this book, therefore, I shall take the field of community development to include any action taken by any agency and primarily designed to benefit the community.

I must make one other preliminary point. Enthusiasts for community development sometimes speak or write about it as if it were something entirely new, and they irritate the very many people who feel that community development is not new, but that its principles were in fact applied by a multitude of individual government officers and missionaries long before anyone had thought of such a term as community development. This is true, and in a very real sense community development as we recognize it today is based on, and has grown out of, the experience of the past. What is new is that these principles are now becoming more widely recognized than ever before, and more consciously and purposefully applied by the many agencies which are basing their policies upon them. It is the emphasis that is new, rather than the principles, and it is all that is implied in this major development—in some cases almost a revolution—in government or agency policy that we now find convenient to term Community Development.[2]

CHAPTER II

TRENDS IN COMMUNITY DEVELOPMENT

BEFORE the Second World War the main emphasis in the development of tropical countries was on communications and material resources. There was much less emphasis on small-scale development specifically related to the needs and welfare of the people in their local communities.

Today the governments of most tropical countries are

aware of the need to foster development in the local community as well as at the national level: and many governments now have special programmes to stimulate and help people to improve their own local way of life. These are known as community development programmes. Nor is interest in such programmes limited to the national governments in the tropics. They have become a main concern of several intergovernmental agencies such as Unesco and the Technical Assistance Committee of the United Nations; while the Point Four programme of the United States, the Ford Foundation's interest in India's Community Projects, and the help given to community development schemes through the United Kingdom's Colonial Development and Welfare Acts illustrate the special interest in this form of development taken by some of the western democracies.

Small communities may, of course, adapt themselves to change and improve their way of life without outside help of any kind, and of this kind of community self-development the Yoruba village of Aiyetoro in Western Nigeria provides an outstanding recent example.[1] But nowadays most small communities do need help to enable them to adjust to the rapid change that goes on all around them. In practice, then, in studying community development, we are concerned with how communities can be developed from without, and by any agency, international or national, government or voluntary.

The small communities in the tropics with which this book is mainly concerned are groups of people—in some cases less than a hundred and at most a few thousands—who live and work together in a village or neighbourhood to which they feel they specially belong. Many of these groups still live in the main according to tradition and inherited custom, and many of them are unprogressive by modern standards. Some have stayed too isolated from the outside world to be much affected by it. Others have held so strongly to their traditional beliefs and customs that they have resisted attempts to change them. Others again have been too ignorant, or too poor, to change their ways without more stimulus, help, and teaching than they have so far had.

One community development problem, then, is *to find effective ways of stimulating, helping, and teaching people to adopt new methods and to learn new skills*: methods and skills which are 'better' than the people's traditional methods and skills because they can help them to grow more food, have better health, and possess more material 'goods' than they have previously enjoyed.

This is only one aspect of community development. In fact, very many small communities *have* accepted change of many kinds. They now grow new crops or improved varieties of crops; they use the plough; they have their cattle inoculated; they send their children to school; and they go out of the community to work for wages. In short, as Professor Firth has said, they show that they have 'a highly expansible set of wants'.

Such changes usually cause new problems. People change their tools but not their methods of farming, and are then threatened with soil erosion. By inoculating their cattle they are able to build up herds which overgraze and finally destroy their pastures. They use the schools to help their children find work in the towns. In short, they accept enough change to upset their traditional way of life without accepting the further changes which would deal with its bad effects. And so, to the first aim of introducing change we now realize that we must add another: *to help people to adapt their way of life to the changes they accept, or have had imposed upon them.*

There is also a third aspect of community development. People in the traditional small community feel that they 'belong', and it is mainly this sense of 'belonging' that keeps them observing community standards of conduct and behaviour. People enforce the accepted group standards on one another. But as change takes place, and new ideas are accepted by some but not by others, or if the old ideas cannot be applied in the new situations brought about by change, standards of conduct tend to become uncertain, the sense of belonging is weakened, and the community may begin to segment or disintegrate. The effects of this may show themselves in various ways: in an increase of crime, such as theft; in a weakening of family relationships; in resistance to traditional authority; in a growth of litigation; in a drift to the towns; in unwillingness to co-operate for the common good; and even in a general bewilderment and apathy. The prevalence of such undesirable symptoms, and a growing awareness of their cause, have begun to make us realize that to encourage material development is to tackle only a part of the community problem. It is at least equally important as change occurs *to ensure that the feeling or spirit of community is not destroyed.*

The idea of community development in the tropics is almost always associated with work in rural areas where recognizable communities already exist. But we are now beginning to recognize a community problem in the many places where economic development has arbitrarily brought together people from many different communities: for example, on plantations, in towns, in industrial areas such as the Northern Rhodesian Copperbelt, and in some rural resettlement areas. Such places collect people out of their rural communities without providing them with any real community in which to live. They present a problem of community development—or more correctly of *community creation*— which has been neglected in most parts of the tropics until quite recently.

While agencies have been broadening their aims they have also been modifying their organization and methods of work. There are several trends. One is for the agencies working in the same area in agriculture, forestry, health, water-supplies, education and so on to plan and work together in a more co-ordinated way than in the past, merging their individual programmes into one overall, well-balanced programme, so that the work of each agency strengthens and complements the work of others. A second trend is to work with groups rather than with individuals 'in the mass', and a third to get people to take as active a part as possible in their community's development. Lastly, more attention is being paid now than in the past to people's customs and beliefs, to their traditional ways of organizing themselves for action, and to their actual *wants* as distinct from the agency's conception of their needs.

There is no set pattern for community development, but the trends mentioned above are today being more consciously and purposefully followed than ever before, and for most people they are what mainly distinguish community development from development of other kinds.

CHAPTER III

AGENCIES AND COMMUNITIES

IT goes without saying that the success or failure of a community development agency will be affected by the community's attitude towards it. Unless this attitude is favourable it is unlikely that the community will act on the agency's advice, or even listen to it.

At the start, the community is influenced more by what the agency has done in the past than by what it is trying to do now. This point is very well illustrated by what happened at Domasi in Nyasaland when a community development agency borrowed an experienced field worker from the forestry department to teach the people how to care for the seedling trees they had planted earlier in the year. We are told that:

In spite of the most careful explanations his tour was taken by some people to be a spying out of local private resources for Government's own purposes ... it was the first time that most of them had met a forestry capitao who was not looking for trouble in the shape of illicit felling or streambank offences. [1]

The people just could not believe that this time the forestry worker had really come to help them.

People will nearly always start with some kind of attitude towards an agency, even if they have no knowledge or experience of what it actually does. They will base their opinion on their experience with some other agency or on hearsay from other communities, and if this is unfavourable the worker will start at a disadvantage, however good his intentions may really be.

Thereafter the community will be confirmed in its original attitude, or will modify it, according to what the worker does and how he actually behaves. That is, everything will depend on the policy of the agency and on the personality, status, and techniques of the worker. Here the foreign worker may sometimes be at a serious disadvantage. He belongs to a different culture. His ideas and customs are different from those of the people among whom he works. He may not speak the language well, and he is likely to think and reason in a different way. He has much to learn before he can work effectively, and other things being equal it would seem that native-born workers are much to be preferred.

However, it must not be overlooked that many native-born workers suffer from most of the disadvantages of the worker from abroad. There is a wide cultural gap between the well-educated, professionally trained, urban-minded expert, native or foreign, and the common people. This is why some agencies prefer to select their workers mainly from people who have a rural background and who are familiar with the ways of country folk. Even if they are less skilled in the technical aspects of their work, they are often better at teaching what they know. It is hard to find enough well-educated people who know and like country people and their ways.

Some agencies try to overcome this difficulty by carefully selecting and training their workers, [2, 3] by instructing them to build up friendly and informal contacts with the people before they begin any specific work, [3, 4] and by leaving them in the same district for a long time so that they can reap full advantage from the friendly relations they gradually establish with the people.

Indeed, it is only when the people come to look on the worker as a friendly and trustworthy person who is working in their interest that he can really begin to function successfully. Even so, he usually has a hard task in the poor and backward areas where development is needed most. And if he fails he is tempted to blame the people. He feels that they must be apathetic, or ultra-conservative, or irrational, or they would not reject the obvious benefits he wants them to accept. If he feels like this he will do well to remember that even illiterate peasants have a keen interest in their own well-being and that they are strictly rational within the limits of their understanding and experience. When they reject the changes he suggests, it is because they see their problems from a different angle.

It is of course a paradox that it is usually the people who have most to gain by changes designed to increase wealth who are the most reluctant to accept them. This is because they of all people can least afford to take risks. They have no reserves to tide them over failure. They know that they can just make a living by doing as they do, and they need to be very sure before they do anything differently. After all, it is they, not the worker, who will suffer if the worker suggests the wrong thing.

However, change does not always seem threatening, even to people who are very poor and backward. They may readily accept a new or better tool or better yielding seed of some existing crop, but even then difficulties may occur and a few examples will help to make this clear.

Some years ago, in 1946, an agricultural extension

worker introduced a new type of hybrid maize into a community of Spanish American farmers in New Mexico. He was already well known and liked. He was able to demonstrate that the new seed yielded three times as much as the seed the farmers normally planted, and he was certain that he was doing right in persuading them to grow it. They followed his advice, but within three years they had nearly all gone back to growing their old low-yielding variety.

This sounds almost incredible, but it can be explained quite simply. The farmers ate the maize they grew. They ground it into flour and with the flour their wives made *tortillas*—the flat round cakes that formed the staple of their diet. But the new type of maize gave a flavour to the cakes the people did not like. The people valued the high yield but did not like the price they had to pay in taste, and the innovation failed because the agency had overlooked the need to test for taste as well as yield before the seed was given to the farmers.[5]

India provides many examples of the same kind. Thus the people of Madhopur rejected a higher-yielding variety of maize because they found that it took so long to ripen that they could no longer double-crop the land where it was sown. The people of a western district of Uttar Pradesh had many good reasons for rejecting improved varieties of wheat. The Government would not allow them to plant it mixed with other grains—a custom they valued because it insured them against complete crop failure when the season was bad for wheat: and it had the further disadvantage that they were expected to repay the borrowed seed by a fixed date regardless of the harvest weather. Nor were these disadvantages the only ones:

The new wheat, when made into bread, tastes flat, and is not nearly so good as the native wheat, mixed as it is with other grains. The women find it difficult to grind the big and tough grains of the new wheat and its dough is hard to knead and bake. The straw is not good for fodder, or for thatching, or for fuel. So great is the cultivator's need for every bit of economic good that can be extracted from the crop that he rightly feels that even small alterations in his precarious over-developed technology may lead to a catastrophe. Using the new seed may rightly seem to many a villager to be a greater gamble than is worth taking.[6]

In all these cases the people understood that by using the 'improved' seed they would increase their yield, but the value of the change in each case was outweighed by disadvantages the agency had not foreseen. The *balance* of advantage was against the innovation. In other cases the people can see no advantage in a suggested change at all. For example, J. H. Driberg relates how he tried to introduce the Canadian double-bladed paddle to a tribe of fishermen in Uganda a good many years ago. He was able to show that it was a better paddle than their own in the sense that it could propel their canoes more quickly, but the tribesmen would not use it, and Driberg tells us why.

For them, he says, their paddles were not just tools for moving boats. They were linked with religion and with magic. They were made from wood prescribed by ritual and charmed by spells to bring good luck in catching fish and to protect their owners from hippopotami and crocodiles. No reasonable fisherman would dream of using a paddle which lacked these all-important qualities, and the Canadian paddle for them, far from being a superior tool, was a much inferior one. Moreover as Driberg points out, it did not fit in with

the tribal technique of paddle-using which the people
had learnt in childhood. For them it was actually clum-
sier than their own. And so he concludes:

in all innovations, as we shall find, a long process of education must precede the introduction of a new idea in order
to make it acceptable to the culture as a whole and to
allow of its ready assimilation.[7]

In stating the need for a long process of education to
precede the introduction of a new idea, Driberg was
thinking of the fishermen, but it may sometimes happen
that the innovators need educating too—educating,
that is, in the need to understand the ideas and the way
of life of the people among whom they work. It is not
enough for an agency worker to be convinced that a
change is good. The people must be convinced too.
Real 'betterment' consists in meeting the people's actual
needs, and these are not always what the agency
initially thinks they are.

We see then the importance of agencies and their
workers studying the people's values, customs, and
beliefs. If they ignore them they risk failure: if they
study them they may win success. Ibn Saud, King of
Saudi Arabia, had already learnt this lesson well when
his religious leaders criticized him for introducing the
telephone. The telephone, they said, was the work of
the devil. Ibn Saud then had the telephone transmit a
verse from the Koran. 'That proved that the telephone
could not be an evil instrument.'[8]

An agency must do more than merely take community needs, customs, values, and beliefs into account.
It must also recognize that all aspects of a traditional
community culture are in some way linked with one
another, and that change in one aspect of the culture

may therefore affect other aspects of it and create new problems. Even the smallest innovation may easily set off a whole series of other changes so that it is often very hard to see what the end result of any change will be. Life in a traditional community is not compartmentalized. Agriculture may be linked with religion, for people may believe that to keep the land fertile and have rain at the right times they must keep the goodwill of their ancestors. It may also be linked to authority, for such goodwill, so people may believe, will depend on the chief performing the appropriate ceremonies at the right times. Even the actual processes of cultivation and the times they are undertaken will be intimately linked with many other aspects of community life, and a new crop or a new tool which seems to be merely a matter of straightforward substitution may have very widespread repercussions.

Such repercussions may or may not have lasting ill effects. Normally a community can adapt itself to them in time. But if it cannot—if the repercussions conflict too strongly with some central concept of the culture which the community cannot or will not change—then it may come under such stress that it may ultimately break up into a mass of disorganized individuals. This is exceptionally well illustrated by the history of the Yir Yoront aborigines of Queensland in Australia.[9]

The Yir Yoronts' most important tool was the stone axe. It was made by the older men who got the axeheads from other aborigines whom they met at the tribal initiation feasts and ceremonies. Each axe remained the property of the man who made it, and the younger men of the kin, the women, and the children, had constantly to ask to borrow it and afterwards return it as they went about their daily tasks. Thus the stone axe emphasized and reinforced in daily life the Yir Yoront values of respect for age, respect for men by women, and the relationships between the kin.

All this was changed when the white people at a near-by mission station brought in steel axes which they traded for work or gave as presents at Christmas time. The aborigines used these steel axes in exactly the same way as their stone axes and for the same purposes. They prized them because they cut better and lasted longer.

But the steel axe unlike the stone one was not a monopoly of the old men. It was the young men, the women, and even the children who most frequently visited the mission station, and for that reason they got the steel axes more easily than the senior males. Wives and children no longer needed to beg an axe from the husband or father. The father had frequently to borrow an axe from them. And although the women and children naturally enjoyed this new state of affairs, they also felt confused and insecure in this new situation. Other changes took place too. 'Ownership became less well defined, so that stealing and trespass were introduced into technology and conduct', and the big initiation feasts became less interesting and less important as the trade in axes dwindled. Moreover, the aborigines could not explain the steel axe and other western innovations in terms of their totemic religion or link them to any of their existing ideas about the world in which they lived. So religion weakened and collapsed and there followed 'an appallingly sudden and complete cultural disintegration and demoralization of the individual such as has seldom been recorded for areas other than Australia. . . . Apathy reigns.'[10]

This is admittedly a very extreme example, but it is useful because it illustrates so clearly how even the simplest change can seriously affect a whole culture. By substituting one material for another in what was essentially the same tool used for the same purposes the Yir Yoronts unwittingly undermined their whole way of life.

What moral can we draw from this? Not, I think, that the aborigines should have been isolated from change and from the anxieties and tensions that change brings, but that there is more to development than successfully introducing any number of separate changes, however good in itself each change may seem to be. 'Development' is achieved only when people are helped to adjust themselves to a whole cluster of related changes. Otherwise the innovating agency may cause the disintegration of the communities in which it works, not their development.

The preceding example shows that beliefs, values, and customs are often so interlinked that when one change is made other changes follow, but some beliefs and values lie nearer to the heart of the community culture than others. While people will often welcome changes in the crops they plant or the tools they use, they can be very resistant to attempts to change the central concepts of their culture. These they will go on struggling to retain long after such innovations as the axe, the plough, and the school have destroyed for ever the old pattern and balance of community life.

The persistence of these core beliefs is well illustrated by the case of a well-educated American Indian who served in the American Army during the war. While he was in the army he learnt about disease and the part germs play in causing it. But this did not shatter the belief in witchcraft which he had learnt as a child from his tribal culture. 'Germs are everywhere,' he reasoned, 'yet only some individuals become susceptible. Why should this be?' His answer was that witchcraft could so weaken a person's resistance as to leave him vulnerable to germs.[11]

Many superstitions which seem demonstrably irrational to the Western scientific mind are so strongly held that no amount of forthright argument and reasoning can change them. One reason may be that they are supported by custom. Thus an American anthropologist writes that Indian peasants in Guatemala have the superstitious belief that if a young person walks in front of an older person, he will become prematurely old. He suggests that this superstition grew out of an exceedingly important principle of Indian social organization, namely, respect for age: that the superstition grew up in support of this principle; and that it is unlikely to be undermined unless support for the idea of respecting age is weakened too.[12]

Another anthropologist has written an illuminating article which deals with this type of problem as it occurs among the Navaho Indians of the United States. He writes about 'covert' or hidden culture, and he defines it as that part of culture which consists of basic, implicit assumptions of which the community itself may be unaware. It is the existence of this covert culture, he says, which explains why the Indians adopt parts of the white American value system without taking over others.[13] Community development agencies need to study the implicit assumptions that influence conduct in the communities in which they work.

Just as the beliefs and customs of people are interlinked and clustered, so also are the people themselves. No community is merely an aggregate of individuals. People belong to groups which have an important influence on their thinking and behaviour. They belong to such formal groups, for instance, as the family and the kin, age-grade and religious groups, and perhaps to co-operative and rural improvement groups as well. They also belong to informal friendship or habit groups made up of people who like each other and spend their leisure in each other's company. One finds such informal groups among the women who gossip at the village well and the men who spend their evening in the village coffee shop. They also exist in towns. They need no special premises of their own and may meet in a back alley or on a street corner. In Calcutta, for example, such groups have always been a feature of street life. They are known as 'addas' and meet under the awnings of the houses.[14]

Both formal and informal groups play an important part in people's lives. They satisfy many social and economic needs and they very largely determine the social status of their members.

Such groups are also important as 'clearing houses' for the exchange of gossip and discussion of ideas, and for this reason the development worker needs to take them into account. When an agency starts work in a community it will itself be a topic of discussion. Opinions will be expressed, and as these harden into group opinion the people's attitude towards the agency will form. Once formed, it will be hard to change, so the agency is wise if it makes sure that enough influential members in all kinds of groups really do understand what its aims are and what it wants to do in the community.[15] The best time to influence group opinion is while it is being formed

Once formed, the group's opinion will greatly influence the attitude and conduct of its individual members, and development workers of every kind must take this into account. This is very clearly brought out by a medical officer of health writing of East Africa:

In matters of sanitary improvement, what the individual thinks is much less important than what the community thinks. For a man to be persuaded to dig a latrine, two things are necessary: firstly, that he should be convinced of its value and of the necessity for having a latrine, and secondly, that he should be reasonably sure that his action will have the approval and preferably the commendation of his neighbours and that it will be free from any chance of ridicule. Fashions provide as strong an impetus to conduct in Africa as in Europe, and fashions exist just as much in sanitary habits as in clothing. It is only by a group approach towards health education that we can hope to create a fashion of hygienic improvements.[16]

This view has been endorsed by experienced workers in many countries and in many fields other than health. Thus Tannous writes of the Arab fellahin:

Social control is strong and effective, and the fellah will hesitate to take a new step independently. In facing such situations individuals manifest their community consciousness through such statements as 'The whole village is for the new idea', 'The village is against this innovation', 'I like what you suggest but I cannot stand against my village'.[17]

It is important, therefore, that the agency should think of interesting and educating whole groups and communities rather than any number of individuals.

CHAPTER IV

SOME PRINCIPLES OF AGENCY WORK

AT the beginning of this book I suggested that community development is the process by which a community adapts itself to change, and that a community development agency is the outside organization that tries to help this process and to speed it up. Then in the previous chapter I examined certain characteristics of the small community that affect its reaction to change, and stressed that the community worker must study these characteristics in each community, draw conclusions from them, and apply them in his work. Some of these conclusions are now well enough established to be regarded as general principles underlying all good community development work, and I want to state them and discuss each of them briefly in this chapter.

1. *The agency must establish friendly and trustful relations with the people whom it hopes to influence*

A worker most easily earns liking and trust by meeting actual wants. For instance, a worker may have to deal with people who keenly want to have their sickness cured, but who are not at all interested in better sanitation, and he will make quicker progress if he is prepared to win the people's confidence with cures before trying to educate them in healthier living. This is supported by experience in many parts of the world. 'Whatever the merits of a public health program based on preventive medicine', says G. M. Foster, 'the fact remains that the average Latin American is interested in doctors and nurses because they can cure his ills.'[1]

An agency must also consider people's feelings, for people who feel criticized find it difficult to learn. Thus however irrational deep-seated customs and beliefs may seem to be it is always unwise to scorn them. But more than this is needed. As an East African agricultural officer has said, success depends on many little things that everybody knows but not everybody thinks of using.

We learn about the more elaborate visual aids: but do we clarify our remarks on tour by drawing in the dust with a stick, or using the blackboard in the village hall? We answer the letters of farmers who ask for advice: but do we always score the first point in the game of winning confidence by doing it without delay? We hope farmers will call at our office to seek advice: but when they come do we always provide them with a comfortable chair and with privacy in which to unburden themselves?[2]

These remarks are based on experience in Uganda, but the spirit of them applies everywhere. In any country and in any kind of community work the worker must be friendly and considerate, not a bureaucrat.

2. *The agency must reach agreement with the people on what the change should be*

There is often a wide gulf between what the agency thinks the community needs and what the community actually wants. This gulf has somehow to be bridged, and most agencies aim to bridge it by educating the community. This is both right and natural, but if such education fails, as it will sometimes do, the reason will not always be that people are unable to understand what they are taught. The teaching may be wrong and the agency itself may need to learn.[3]

And after all, that is only to be expected. Professional agency workers plan for communities in which they do not live: and while they can often diagnose a general need for a whole area, specific ways of meeting it need working out afresh in each community. Every community is in some way different from every other and the pre-planned solution hardly ever fits without some detailed alteration. Even neighbouring communities have different histories, different personalities as their leaders, different physical environments, and differences in local skills and resources. No specific change is *a priori* good for a community. It must be tried and tested, and adapted to its special needs and circumstances. Even a fertilizer adopted by one community will be rejected in another (poorer) one because it costs too much.[4]

The agency which studies each local community can anticipate this kind of difficulty, but it needs to study the beliefs, values, and customs of the community as well as its resources. People do not easily change long-standing habits, and agencies need to take this into account. For instance, people who have been accustomed to satisfying their bodily needs out-of-doors will more readily accept an unroofed privy than a roofed one, and a 'seat' privy will probably be rejected by people who squat.

It is also useful sometimes to link suggestions to established values. The Masai cattle-herders of East Africa despise manual work and usually employ men of other

tribes to do it, so that when a water shortage threatened
and the administration wanted to pipe water to their
cattle, they refused to help, although no other labour
was available. They were only persuaded when the
administration finally managed to link the project
firmly enough to their overriding love of cattle. True, it
was not good that the Masai warriors should demean
themselves with manual work: their work lay with their
cattle. But this *was* work for cattle. Would they rather
lose them? or save them by working on the pipe? Put
in this way the real issue became clear and the major
value prevailed.

Occasionally, it is helpful to link an innovation with
beliefs. The instance of Ibn Saud and the telephone has
been mentioned already (p. 13). Tannous mentions its
value with the Arab fellahin when he says that an
appropriate quotation from the Koran is sometimes the
most convincing argument a worker can use to support
a new idea or project.[5] Similarly, an appropriate text
from the Bible is said to have the same convincing effect
in some of the rural communities of the United States.

3. *The agency must demonstrate that a suggested change is safe*

Many extension workers, social workers, and group
workers prejudice their chances of success because they
neglect this principle. The worker must always make
people feel safe against the risk of exposing their ignorance or being ridiculed, while in extension work in poor
and backward areas he must also make them feel that
it is *materially* safe to accept the suggested change.

When there is very little surplus of subsistence, as among
many of the cultivators of India, the taking over of new
seeds, new tools, new techniques may appear as a possibly

catastrophic gamble, with too slender resources urged by an uncomprehending outsider. New technical processes very often demand a period of experimentation by the villager before he can adapt them to his local conditions. Many in India simply cannot afford the experimental period if it threatens the yield of a single harvest.[6]

What is true of the Indian villager is true also of every peasant who lives at or near the subsistence level, and what is true of agriculture applies equally to health and other aspects of community life. In such situations the agency must be able to reassure people, and it is the great weakness of the government demonstration farm that however successfully it may grow new crops it will often fail to convince the peasant that he can do the same. The government farm is not run by peasants but by trained men, and it is backed by government funds. The peasant can call on but little labour and even less money, and quite reasonably he is unimpressed. 'These things are all right for the government,' he says, 'but not for me.'

He is more likely to accept new crops and new methods when he has seen them used by people like himself, and this is why some agricultural agencies teach by sponsoring one or two farmers in each community, and if necessary guarantee them against loss while they try out the new crops or methods. If they are successful others will usually want to try them too.[7]

4. *The agency must be interested in working with groups*

Most people are greatly influenced by group opinion, and for this reason it is often better to try to influence groups than to attempt to win over numbers of people as individuals. But groups vary in size, solidarity, status in the community, and in the purposes and interests of their members. Internally, they differ in the kind of relationships their members have with one another. The members themselves differ in status and in the amount of influence they have. Some groups are dominated by a single leader: in others, leadership is shared.

Knowing its groups helps the agency to find the best way to approach them and the best way to introduce a suggested change. It needs to know which people and groups are likely to support it and which to oppose it, and for what reasons.

People may resist a change for reasons quite unconnected with the nature of the change proposed. More especially, those people will oppose it who feel their status threatened. Every small community grants status to its experts: to the elders as authorities on custom; to the old women for their reputed skill as midwives; and to the healer or witchdoctor for his skill in curing their disease. Yet nearly every innovation threatens, or seems to threaten, the status of some influential people of this kind, and it is their reaction to the threat they feel to their security that often makes attempts at innovation fail.

Such danger can often be avoided by working with them rather than against them. This usually means that the community worker will thoroughly discuss his ideas with the elders and win their approval before he contacts other groups in the community. Then more specifically, e.g. in health programmes, he will contact the community's own 'health experts', make friends with them, and try to work *through* them, and in that way safeguard their status. He will try to avoid giving the impression that he wants to bring in his own agency's workers to supplant them. Child welfare workers in

Formosa found it as necessary to work with the mothers-in-law of the young married women as with the young married women themselves.

Clearly no agency can apply these principles effectively unless it is keenly interested in every aspect of community life. It is not enough for it to study the people's material needs. Such studies only suggest what is theoretically desirable, and in practice many other factors must be taken into account. The intrinsic merits of any proposed change may count for little in the face of doubt about the agency's real purpose, fear of the unknown, and local enmities and rivalries. Many useful innovations have been rejected solely on emotional grounds.

CHAPTER V

DIRECTING CHANGE

THERE are two main kinds of development agency: the one which tries to introduce specific changes and is mainly interested in material development; and the other which is primarily interested in people. On the whole the first wants to 'get things done'; the other to develop the people's own abilities for leadership, wise judgement, and co-operative action. For agencies of this second kind the material result is less important than the way it is achieved.

Agencies and workers who themselves decide the

specific form development should take assume, of course, that they know better than the people what the people need. Most missionaries and government officers have worked on this assumption until quite recently, and although they were often right they were not always right, for they sometimes made the mistake of assuming that what was good within their own culture was certain to be good in other cultures too. Missionaries, for instance, insisted on their converts wearing clothes because they were used to them themselves, and they established schools with syllabuses that suited the missionaries' own countries, rather than the countries where the schools were built.

Agencies and their workers tend to be more careful nowadays, but experts and specialists trained in Western ways still often make mistakes in cultures other than their own.[1] Thus at a recent conference on technical assistance to Asian countries representatives from southeast Asia all felt

. . . that much of the technical assistance rendered by various agencies over the last few years had been at least ineffective, and often positively harmful, because it was based on the export from the West of material and technique designed to produce measurable results quickly, and operated by 'experts' more familiar with techniques than sensitive to situations . . . experts who knew the answers before they got there were no use at all.[2]

In fact, agencies everywhere are now realizing that they are risking failure if they assume that their own ideas are right in environments and cultures other than their own. The East African Groundnut Scheme failed because it did not take the local conditions of soil and climate sufficiently into account. The West African

Anchau Rural Development Scheme illustrates, less spectacularly, the result of failing to consider the human factor when working in a different culture.

This Scheme was started in 1937 to eradicate sleeping sickness from a part of the Zaria province of the Northern Region of Nigeria. There was to be a fly-free corridor about seventy miles long by about ten miles wide, and some 60,000 people living in the surrounding area were to be moved into it.

The men in charge made a detailed survey. They plotted every stream, every tributary, every hamlet, every well, every path, and every trade route. They made a careful census of the people. They made detailed studies of farming conditions in sample hamlets. They made vegetation surveys, water-table surveys, water consumption surveys, and fuel consumption surveys in order to know where to pick good sites for the proposed new villages. Indeed, they scientifically examined in minute detail every aspect of their problem that seemed to them important.

They also developed a positive economic programme. They aimed at increasing the quality of the livestock and the supply of manure for spreading on the farms. They marked out areas of communal forest and demarcated forest reserves. In addition, they used the Sleeping Sickness Ordinance to compel the people to clear the stream banks near their villages with unpaid labour.

What do we see if we try to assess all this activity? We get a picture of a highly-trained group of experts co-operating in a scheme wholly designed for the benefit of people living in an area heavily infected with sleeping sickness, and badly in need of help. And though to them the problem was primarily a health problem, they recognized that it could only be properly dealt with by studying and modifying many aspects of the economic life of the communities for whom they worked. In all these ways the Scheme marked a great advance on normal pre-war government administrative practice.

What other characteristics are especially noteworthy? We can find one in the care devoted to the preparation of very detailed plans based on the facts collected during the survey, but we must note also that all this planning went on solely inside the heads of the government officers concerned. They fixed their goals in carefully planned detail, and then worked hard to turn their plans into real achievement in terms of villages built to these plans and villagers behaving in accordance with the requirements of the plans. And when we ask how people were got to behave as the plans required, the Report[3] on the Scheme gives us the unmistakable impression that this means was power. In practice, the Scheme appears to have been put across by the government officers letting it be clearly understood that their plans must go through, and that it would be far easier for the villagers if they conformed than if they did not.

'Trouble', writes the author of the Report, 'was only experienced with the people of Kudumi, Pegi, and Yelwa villages who ran away into Kano Emirate. They were eventually brought back and made to settle in their new villages. When they realized that there was no alternative they settled down extremely well. . . .'

And again,

The townsmen from old Anchau have proved far more intractable than the peasants, and have the typical, but understandable, slum dwellers' mentality; even though they require much stronger handling, they are at last settling down. . . .

It was not until 1945 that a propaganda team was formed of four trained men and an Emir's representative who toured every village in the Corridor 'with excellent results'.

In general, while reading the Report, one gets the impression that the people were thought of as being there 'to be done good to' in the mass, but that they were not envisaged as *persons*, each with his own small world of hopes and fears, who might in some way be consulted. Nor were different community 'personalities' recognized. All were expected to conform to the same blue-print. The Hausa peasant, we are told, has 'the mentality of a likeable but lazy schoolboy, who will shirk every task until he is made to realize that it must be done, and then he will do it quite cheerfully'.

Finally, let us note what the officer-in-charge has to say about results after the first ten years of work. He is quite frank. If Europeans left the Corridor some good would live on, but few of the people would keep to the new standards.

'Unless', he says, 'the Anchau Corridor has continuous supervision whilst a competent Native Administration is being trained, it will certainly slip back . . . at least one officer from our staff will be needed for a considerable number of years.'

So much for Anchau. This last quotation brings out clearly the weakness of the directive approach which relies mainly on power. It is basically costly and inefficient, and this is sometimes recognized even by those who would prefer to work in this way. Thus Apostolos

Koskinides, one of H. B. Allen's ablest community
workers in pre-war Macedonia, can write:

There would be no objection whatsoever to the use of coercion in rural areas if its use could ensure permanent benefits. But it has been tried in many places without success. . . .
A program based on coercion requires a large personnel to
enforce all the rules and regulations, and this makes it far
too expensive. If it were possible to secure results at a
reasonable cost by this means, the sanitary conditions in
all countries would be much better than they are today.[4]

The lengths to which an unwilling people will go to
maintain custom and resist change forced upon them
by an outside power is well illustrated by Mekki Abbas
in a report on the development of rural communities in
the Sudan.[5] He mentions that in several cases Arabs
who were forced to build mud houses in a new village
to replace their tents were then found to have erected
their tents inside their new mud houses.

It is because so often power is an ineffective and
costly means of introducing change that many agencies
—even those most certain of the rightness of their aims
—have sought other and more efficient means of
changing community values and community customs.

One obvious way is to get the support of the community's leaders, for if they can be won over the
chances are that the rest of the community will follow.
This is the principle adopted by the American Soil Conservation Service, but it was found that in the more
homogeneous communities the natural leaders, i.e. the
people to whom other people defer and whose example
they are willing to follow, are those who most strongly
identify themselves with the existing customs. Such
'leaders', writes one critic,

. . . may actually help to freeze a situation which must be broken somehow before agricultural innovations are widely accepted. Some such leaders may need to be discovered, not as the SCS analysis would have it, in order to employ them like Moses in leading their people out of a prescientific wilderness into the technological 'promised land'—but rather in order to neutralize their influence as living embodiments of an outmoded culture.[6]

So in first approaching the leaders in such groups, the agency may in fact be approaching the most resistant members of the community, and what is true of America is in this instance just as true of Asia and Africa. It is easy to find parallels for such leaders among the illiterate elders of many Asian and African rural communities.

Alternatively, the agency can approach the individuals in the community who seem to be most willing to consider new ideas. This approach also has some disadvantages. In the really homogeneous community 'deviants' of this kind are likely to be few, and what is more important, they are unlikely to have much influence over others. The people who are usually most willing to accept ideas rejected by the rest are those who for some reason have least to lose by launching out on their own. They are either exceptionally ambitious or they are people of low status who are seeking any means of improving it. Such people do not provide good channels for new ideas to enter the community. People do not ordinarily adopt new customs from people of lower status than themselves.

This is not the only disadvantage of concentrating on receptive individuals regardless of the community status they enjoy, for success with this method may cause a split in the community between the few 'progressives' and the larger 'unprogressive' group. Thereafter, the harder and more successfully the agency works with its minority of progressives, the wider will yawn the economic and social gulf between them and the rest— and the smaller will be the chance of the new ideas getting across to the larger, backward group. This appears to be the great weakness, for example, of the peasant farming project in the eastern province of Northern Rhodesia.[7] There, so I have been told, the 'progressive' farmers are 'progressively' cutting themselves off from their communities, challenging the authority of their traditional leaders, and seeing themselves and their interests more and more clearly as separate and distinct from those of their fellows. In a very real sense this is the negation of community development. This same problem is recognized in the 'Report on Rural Community Organization and Development in the Caribbean Area and Mexico'[8] which states (p. 4):

Instances were observed in which a number of specialized technical agencies were each using sub-groups, quite often groups which they themselves had promoted, and by this practice were segmenting communities rather than developing programmes in which all local residents were to some extent participating.

Agencies, therefore, that aim at influencing *all* the people of an area—at remoulding them, as it were, better to fit the agencies' ideas of what is good for them —have to face the problem of trying to influence and instruct whole communities rather than any number of separate and distinct individuals: and during the last few years many new methods and new techniques have been designed with this in mind.

One useful and badly needed advance has been the development of better techniques of co-operation between different agencies working in the same area. This is important for two reasons. Agency rivalries can segment communities, as we have just seen: and they can also lead to duplication, conflict, and waste of effort and resources. Lord Hailey mentions this problem. 'The absence of co-ordination', he says, 'is seen most markedly in such departments as those of health, sanitation, agriculture, or veterinary work. Departments tend to trench on each other's field of work, with the result that there is not only overlapping but even, at times, a conflict of policy.'[9]

The same problem exists almost everywhere. Thus in Ceylon, in one and the same village, one may find the Agricultural Department sponsoring Young Farmers' Clubs, the Rural Development Department sponsoring rural development societies, the Co-operative Department sponsoring co-operative credit societies, and the Local Government Department sponsoring community centres. A Cingalese community worker tells me that this multiplicity of societies has often become a real nuisance to the village people, and that rivalry between the departments sponsoring the different societies has tended to accentuate existing factions in the villages.

There has been a similar problem in Egypt, where the three Ministries of Public Health, Social Affairs, and Agriculture have each embarked on programmes for improving rural health:[10] and it has existed, too, in Puerto Rico, where four different agencies have each employed their own village workers on very similar kinds of work among the same people.

Several ways of solving this problem have been tried. One is the organization of officers of administrative and technical departments in 'teams' on a district, provincial, or area basis: and another, the idea of employing village level workers. Each of these workers is stationed in a group of about fifteen villages where he acts as the local representative of all rural development departments. The idea of the team is especially associated with British territories in Africa, and that of the general village level worker with Community Projects in India.

Members of District or Area Teams work closely together in framing programmes and plans for all kinds of rural development, and they produce a combined plan for their whole district. The operation of such a team in a Kenya district has been well described by Fergus Wilson. In his article[11] we note the same stress as in Anchau on the gathering of information and careful preliminary planning, but there is distinctly more emphasis than in the Anchau Scheme on the need to involve African local authorities and African technical assistants by encouraging them to suggest minor amendments. Propaganda is also given more skilful and careful attention than it received at Anchau.

Perhaps it is in Uganda that propaganda has been most effectively harnessed to the work of the district team: for in Uganda there are special Demonstration Teams which are designed to put across, in the most effective way possible, any points that the district teams may wish to emphasize. The Demonstration Team is not a team of specialists employed by the various departments. Members of such teams are specialists only in the sense that they are specialists in propaganda. They are briefed as required in the details of the programme they are to take to the people, and they work out, as a team, just how they can best present it to make the maximum impact.

Work of this kind in conjunction with the Health Department has been well described by Dr. R. G. Ladkin in an article on 'Health Education in Buganda',[12] and more generally by G. A. R. Savage in an article on 'The Use of a Demonstration Team in Community Development'.[13]

Savage defines the Demonstration Team as an extension agency for the district team. He describes a typical campaign to teach soil conservation, cotton planting, the construction of pit latrines, and the protection of springs.

The first stage is the holding of a Local Leaders' Course for 'chiefs, council members, school teachers, prominent farmers, and so on'. The course consists of lectures; demonstrations; a static exhibition of posters, photographs and models; visits; practical work; and discussion. After the leaders have been briefed and have returned to their villages, the Demonstration Team then tours the whole area and spends three or four days in each village. During this time it gives concerts and playlets which in some way or another underline the lessons the campaign is designed to teach. It shows films; sets up its exhibitions; organizes practical work on its projects; and promotes discussion at village meetings. Always, the content of instruction is put over in many different ways and with much emphasis on visual and dramatic methods. When the team has gone, its teachings are followed up by departmental field workers helped by the local people who had attended the special leaders' course and by one or more members detached from the Demonstration Team for the purpose.

The Demonstration Team approach is good in several ways. It is the agent of the district team rather than of any one technical department, and thus it is a practical means of reducing inter-departmental conflicts and rivalries in the field. But it has other uses too. It is easier, one may believe, for even a conservative leader to open his mind to new ideas when he meets them away from his own community on a Local Leaders' Course, and especially when they are presented to him in so many different ways. Nor is he likely to resist because he feels his status threatened, for this is recognized in the title of the Course itself.

It is worth noting, too, that in its talks, demonstrations, concerts, and plays, the Team puts its message into the local idiom and links it with community values and beliefs. Community customs are treated with respect. The people are encouraged in every way to take part in the process by which they learn, and in ways sanctioned by existing custom. Thus in Buganda the Team appeals to the old Buganda custom of 'bulungibwansi', or work for the community, when getting the people to do practical work on its projects. The aim is always to reduce the need for power by creating a local social atmosphere and local social pressures favourable to the desired change, and thus to make it easy for individuals to change their behaviour in the ways desired.

At best, however, the Demonstration Team approach can only stimulate temporarily. By itself it is unlikely to have much permanent effect, and it is for this reason that the idea of having an all-purpose village level worker is important. In India, where this idea has been applied on a very large scale, the ideal is to have one such worker for each small group of villages. There in his own area his first job, so we are told, is to get known, liked, and trusted by the village people and to become thoroughly well acquainted with their customs, beliefs, village organization, and material environment. Only then is he to begin to develop projects through discussion—plenty of discussion—with the villagers. During discussion he will introduce knowledge and ideas which are new to the villagers, and he will sponsor as tactfully as possible the aims that his agency has for the development of the village. During discussion, too, he will acquire information about the wants and needs of the villagers which he will pass back to his supervisor, together with requests for specialized technical assistance and advice whenever they are needed. Such requests will be met by the supervisor calling in staff from the appropriate technical departments. Above all, it is stressed that the village-level worker must live and work among the villagers, identifying himself with them in work and recreation in every possible way.

But why then discuss the Indian village worker in a chapter on 'directing change'? The reason is that, as one reads the literature and talks with Indians, one realizes that in India one is near the borderline between the agency directing change and the agency assisting change to happen. In India the rural development problem is so big, and in the eyes of the Indian leaders so urgent, that the village workers have to show results, and show them quickly. Whatever the ideal may be, the real aim is for material development, and for the kinds of material development that the government wants: and where this cannot be fostered quickly enough by purely permissive educational methods, pressure and more directive methods are often used. Whenever this happens the villagers see the village level worker as yet another government officer appointed to inflict the purposes of government upon them, rather than to help them; and the workers still see the villagers as apathetic or resistant. Thus in *Kurukshetra*, the monthly journal of Indian Community Projects, there is a description of a visit by a group of university students to help the villagers in a project area. In one village the project was the building of a girls' school, but hardly any villagers would work. The Assistant Project Officer asked the headman why the villagers did not come to work, since they wanted the school. 'We do not want a girls' school,' said the headman. 'What is the use of educating girls? Who would bring our midday meal to the fields if the girls went to school?'[14]

In a neighbouring village a child welfare centre had been built but was left unused. 'Who washed our eyes in childhood? Are our eyes weak?' asked the old women. It is evident that in this area, at least, communities were being pressed into projects that were not in any real sense community projects.

It is easy for community workers to fall into errors of this kind whenever they are working among people who have habitually avoided trouble with the authorities by superficially doing what they are told. In such areas communities will build a clinic or a school, not because they want it, but to stop the government worker worrying them. They try to buy him off, as it were, by providing what he seems to want, but with no intention of permanently altering their existing ways. Thus it is easier to get them to build a school or clinic than to use it or maintain it.

I saw a good example of this in West Africa a year or two ago when I was taken to see a village hall which, I was informed, had been built by the villagers as 'a community project'. The hall was quite a good one, but

I was puzzled by its situation, for it was sited some distance from the village. I asked the village headman why it had been built, and he replied, quite simply, 'For the government.' That was how the villagers saw it and, indeed, that was the truth, for the hall was used as a government tax collection centre but not for local community activities of any kind.

Near by was a fine and hygienic, cement-lined well which the villagers had helped to build, also as 'a community project', but they had not trodden a path to it and did not use it.

In reality, the village hall and the well, though officially listed as community projects, were nothing of the kind. They were *government* projects to which the people had agreed to give their labour. They had never been accepted by the people as projects of their own, and no one in the community was interested in using or maintaining them. Such projects do not constitute community development or, indeed, development of any kind.

We have now seen the directive agency using approaches of several different kinds, varying from the obviously directive and authoritaiian methods of Anchau to the informal and friendly approach of the Indian village level worker. Basicaliy, however, all these agencies face the same problem—how to get the people to conform to what the government wants if the people do not really want it too. In such circumstances if the agency wants quick results it must use pressure and go on using it or the people will slip back into their old ways. The alternative is community education, but this is apt to be a slow process, and the temptation to press on with change too fast is very real. The results of doing so, even under very favourable conditions, are strikingly illustrated by the pilot project in community development on Moturiki. [15]

This project was carried out in 1951 and 1952 on a small island in the Fiji group in the Pacific. It was tried under ideal conditions. No fewer than seven workers were posted to the project for two whole years although there were only 588 men, women, and children on the island. The island itself was divorced from normal administrative control so as to leave the project team entirely free to work unhampered by routine administration. The people welcomed the project as likely to increase their status and were stimulated by many visits from high-ranking government officials. The project team itself was carefully selected and specially trained, and supported by relatively large funds in view of the very small size of the population: and it was supported, too, by a Headquarters Advisory Group which included the directors of the Education, Health, and Agricultural Departments as well as the District Commissioner South and a member of the Fijian Affairs Board.

The project started with a survey of conditions and resources on the island as a preliminary to the planning of development and the training of the team, but (my italics):

It was unfortunate that the one project suggested by the villagers themselves, village amalgamation, had, after very careful consideration, to be postponed owing to the immense and exclusive demand it would make on man-power.

However, many other development projects were planned for agriculture, health, education, forestry, and housing, and there were many activities specially designed for women. A local Development Committee was formed, and during the next sixteen months the people did a great deal of useful work under the guidance and stimulus exerted by the team.

The team was withdrawn at the end of 1951, and Mr. Hayden gives details of what happened during 1952. The Development Committee lost interest; agriculture and forestry on the whole 'slipped back to the pre-Project time', the carpentry and pit-sawing projects came to an end; the boys' camp no longer flourished; and the school uniform and school milk schemes were abandoned. On the other hand, the people continued with the copra and firewood selling schemes; they started a co-operative society; they continued to support the clinic; and the women's craft work continued to flourish. But the team had failed, so we are told, to develop local leadership or to stimulate local initiative. The islanders accepted selling schemes that provided them with cash, but neglected nearly all the other innovations except the clinic. They had subscribed to this through their Development Fund, and it was now staffed by a resident nurse for whom the government paid.

Thus after two years' work most of the team's projects were still 'government' projects as far as the people were concerned. They did not see why they should build houses, carry gravel and plant rice 'for the government' without pay. And if the government wanted them to use sea latrines the Public Works Department should make them.[16] Thus most of the projects never did become the people's projects. They lapsed when the team went and the pressure was removed, and Howard Hayden comments:

. . . it would appear essential, in any large campaign using the team technique, to allow for a series of return visits to be made by all the members of the Team over a considerable period of time, and particularly for the Team leader to be accessible for consultation after he has moved to another development area.[17]

This is, indeed, curiously reminiscent of T. A. M. Nash's summing up in the Anchau Report. It illustrates once again the real weakness of the directive approach: and one wonders whether the authorities might not have discovered more local leadership and initiative if they had allowed the people to go ahead with their village amalgamation project. After all, people are more likely to take the lead in carrying through projects of their own.

Although every directive agency selects its own targets for the community and is therefore likely to come up against the same problem, better ways of dealing with it are being found. Most agencies now study their communities before they choose their targets; and more and more agencies are studying community values and customs, community leadership and community social structure, as well as the community's resources and environment. If such studies are carefully and sympathetically made they inevitably bring the agency closer to the people. They provide the knowledge that helps the agency to select the most appropriate targets and to present them in ways that the people can best appreciate and understand. In addition, agencies are learning that people co-operate more willingly when they feel that they have a real share in deciding what should be done and how it should be done, as well as in doing it.

The Kigezi Resettlement Scheme, Uganda, provides an almost perfect example of these newer methods of directing change. The Kigezi country was over-populated and over-cultivated, and many people had to be moved away. It was decided, however, that resettlement was to be entirely voluntary. Any form of forced resettlement was to be avoided.

Thus from the first the district staff had to face what was primarily an educational problem, and J. W. Purseglove, the Agricultural Officer concerned, stresses that the first step was to concentrate on a general, intensive propaganda which pointed out the evils of over-population.[18] It took eighteen months to convince the senior chiefs that some measure of resettlement was really in the interests of the people, and when this happened the next step was to go with them to look over possible resettlement areas with a view to choosing the best. These chiefs happened to be 'natural' as well as 'institutional' leaders, and from the first they were intimately involved, even at the planning stage. Then, when the area had been chosen, volunteers were called for to go out with the chiefs to view the promised land 'but without any obligation that they would subsequently emigrate'. Lorry transport was provided and buffalo meat shot for them. Purseglove goes on to say:

Of my first party of 100 volunteers, 51 took up land. Of my second party . . . the whole party of 125 took up land within four days of leaving their old homes. It was very exciting to go round and see knots in the grass, slashes on trees, and poles marking the new boundaries of land which had been taken up.

In all this, and in the developments which followed, there was no regimentation. There were no minutely detailed plans like those of Anchau; the aim was to create a genuine permissive atmosphere, to ease difficulties by alleviating genuine hardship, and to avoid spoon-feeding. At the same time a big educational programme in land utilization was begun, with courses for chiefs, agricultural staff, and teachers on the Agricultural Department's experimental farm.

This resettlement operation proved so successful that it was several times necessary to hold back intending settlers while those who had most recently moved were being settled in. By 1950 the resettlement area was already nearly full and presented, in Purseglove's own words, 'a picture of a settled community in an area which three years ago was merely the home of big game'. It was an impressive achievement. There was certainly betterment, there was plenty of active participation, and we are told that the people were left free to co-operate in the scheme or not as they wished.

Though we should give full credit to the organizers of the Kigezi Scheme, we should also recognize that they had a relatively clear-cut task, for the core of their problem was simply to get enough people to agree to move away from their overcrowded lands to a new settlement area, that is, to get enough people to make one big decision. But most attempts at community development are far more complex than this and call rather for a continuous exercise of local initiative and leadership in many small matters, and this is much harder for the community worker to stimulate.

This is well illustrated by a pre-war community development scheme in Macedonia.[19] The scheme was a gem of its kind. The Americans who were in charge of it showed quite outstanding patience, tact, and kindliness, and a real capacity for making friends with the villagers they were trying to help. Not surprisingly, therefore, they were able to initiate many schemes of agricultural and home improvement, and by all short term standards they were exceptionally successful.

Their work came to an end when the Germans over-ran the Balkans during the Second World War and has not been resumed since, but an American sociologist visited the area in 1950 to assess what permanent results had been achieved.[20] He writes that the villagers remember the scheme with approval, and that they remember what they were taught and still practise some of it—most where it helped them to improve their economic position: least in relation to home improve-ment and child welfare. He is satisfied that the villagers would like the scheme to be resumed. Youth clubs, he says, could easily be started where young farmers' clubs had previously existed, and the villagers are ready to resume the pre-war committee and planning procedure.

At first sight this report seems eminently satisfactory. Some changes, together with a social climate favourable to a resumption of extension work, had persisted for at least ten years, half of which were years of war. But is it really so satisfactory? The general impression is still one of a static community, willing indeed to be moulded and stimulated, but without initiative and leadership of its own. One wonders whether the workers on the original scheme may not have stressed too much what was needed for getting quick, practical results, and too little the encouragement of local initiative and a local responsible leadership, which could go on producing results long after the scheme had ended. How else can we explain the present passivity of the villagers so that they wait for people from outside to restart their youth clubs and committees? Should not one of the prime tests —the prime test in fact—of community development be the emergence of local leaders willing to take initiative and able to exercise responsibility, and the emergence of groups, clubs, and committees which local people control and through which they act to achieve purposes of their own? In the last analysis, the community worker succeeds in so far as he succeeds in making himself redundant.

A purist arguing from this standpoint would maintain that none of the directive schemes and projects described in this chapter really contributed very much to community development just because all real initiative remained with the agencies. There is, however, a good deal to be said on the other side. Most agencies do, in fact, regard these projects as community development, and there are many more rural development projects of this directive kind than of the type that stresses first and foremost the growth among the people of independent judgement, free leadership and initiative. There are many reasons for this. Most governments want quick results, and this means reaching specific targets within a given time. Moreover, in many situations, directing change may be the only—and therefore the best—way of helping a community. This is true of nearly all crisis situations where speed is essential: where, for instance, severe soil erosion threatens the people's future livelihood, or where preventible disease has made them too apathetic to be helped in any other way. But when all this is said, there is no doubt that many agencies do direct too much. Directive methods are in the government administrative tradition and they are temptingly straightforward and easy to apply.

There is, however, a strong case for encouraging people more often to think out targets for themselves while tactfully trying to educate them to choose their targets wisely. It is only in this way, slow and uncertain as it may often be, that the agency can stimulate a really constructive local leadership and initiative. As this develops the people will begin to develop their own community instead of always having development thrust upon them. To stimulate this kind of development the agency must work *with* people rather than *for* them. It means slower work but often gives more lasting results. It is not enough to get people to participate in the agency's projects. The ideal is that the people should adopt their own.

CHAPTER VI

AIDING COMMUNITY PROJECTS

MANY people would not agree that the kind of agency work discussed in the previous chapter can rightly be called community development. Community development, they would say, properly includes only those kinds of development which are freely chosen and undertaken by local communities for themselves, and they would agree with the authors of the United Nations Report on Rural Community Organization and Development in the Caribbean Area and Mexico who write:

In all the cases seen, where real progress was being accomplished in local community development, the first step in that development had been sustained discussion by the community of its basic needs and most urgent problems. Progress in development had followed a fairly easily-recognized pattern. First, the people of the community, generally, if not always, stimulated by a 'group organizer' or

'Extension Teacher', had become aware of one or more common problems by sustained or repeated discussion. Second, they had, as a group, decided to accept the responsibility of pooling their intelligence, manpower, and local resources to attack one *specific* problem, the solution of which would meet some felt need of a large majority or all the families in the community. Third, they organized to solve that problem and, in every case studied, learned that they needed some specialized assistance and, in practically all cases, some material or financial assistance from outside the community. Fourth, they developed a degree of group responsibility, pride, and zest which led them on to attack other community problems. [1]

This idea of community development confronts the agency with problems of a different kind from those discussed in the last chapter. The agency does not sponsor any specific targets of its own. Its task is to make communities interested and active in developing themselves, in finding and choosing targets, in making and executing plans, and in maintaining and using the results of those plans when the targets—roads, markets, village halls, clean water-supplies, or whatever they might be—have been successfully completed.

These objectives demand new techniques. The prime object of the agency is to help people to find out what they would like to do and how best they can do it for themselves. The agency has no pre-fixed, specific targets of its own, and it is less concerned with teaching and instructing people than with helping them to learn. The agency worker, therefore, does not direct the community or lead it. He acts mainly as a catalyst, encouraging people to think for themselves. As a teacher he serves whatever aims the people have or may develop.

This idea is a relatively new one, and many agencies

find it both practicable and attractive. It is practicable wherever the work of government officers, missionaries, and traders has already made people so conscious of new wants that with a little encouragement they are willing to do something about them for themselves. It is attractive partly because it is cheap, for in this sort of development, labour, local materials, and sometimes money are provided by the people. It is also attractive because the successful project raises community morale and makes the people more receptive to new ideas. Thus by aiding community projects the agency develops a favourable climate for introducing its own projects in the future. Meanwhile it is assisting a form of local development which makes only a small demand on its own limited resources.

One of the best-known and earliest examples of community development of this kind occurred among the Ibo in the Udi division in south-eastern Nigeria.[2] There small, rather backward, and largely illiterate communities—stimulated originally by a mass literacy project in 1944—have undertaken all kinds of local projects which they have selected for themselves. Thus many small Ibo communities have provided themselves with schools, reading-rooms, co-operative shops, markets, maternity centres, clean water-supplies, and even leper villages, by means of their own labour and money resources. They have been encouraged by government administrative officers, but they have been given only a little outside help. This has usually taken the form of cement or pan for roofing, or the temporary loan of a skilled mason or carpenter.

It was largely due to the striking success of the community project in the Udi division that the idea soon spread to other parts of Nigeria and to

Ghana,* but it has not everywhere been as successful as at Udi. There are good reasons for this, for conditions at Udi were exceptionally favourable to project work. The people still retained their strong sense of community solidarity, for their lives had not been much upset by economic change. At the same time they had been brought into touch with new ideas, for some of their young men had been attracted out of their rural communities to work in the Enugu coal-mines near by. From them the people had learned new wants. What happened, therefore, was that the people adapted their traditional custom of working for the community to new and untraditional goals.

If local circumstances at Udi were exceptionally favourable to community project work, so also was the personality and drive of the local administrative officer. He was well known, liked, and trusted by the Udi people, and he encouraged them in every possible way. He gave desirable schemes his blessing; he spread the project idea by spreading the news of successful projects to other villages; he visited the villages during the course of their project work; and he readily arranged whenever possible to provide technical advice, technical help, and materials which the people could not provide out of their own local resources.

It is this last factor—the personal interest and encouragement of some government officer well qualified by aptitude or training for this kind of work—that is all important: for West African communities will rarely proceed with any project, except, perhaps, a church, unless they are first stimulated by a government officer

* In March, 1957, the people of the Gold Coast renamed their country 'Ghana', and it is by this name only that it is everywhere referred to in this book.

and are sure of government support. In Ghana this condition is met by the numerous field staff of the Department of Social Welfare and Community Development. In Nigeria, where there is no comparable department, it is one of the many duties of the administrative officer; and the marked variation in the number and quality of village projects in neighbouring divisions and provinces is partly to be explained by differences in the interest and skill of the administrative officers concerned.[3]

Even under favourable conditions, as at Udi, the project worker must be patient and skilful to obtain the best results. Desirably, the community should choose a project that meets a real local need, and plan it on an appropriate scale. To say this, of course, is merely to state the obvious, but it needs stating, for communities do not always tackle projects solely with their usefulness in mind. If projects are 'in the fashion', and especially if a community has been stimulated by news of what neighbouring communities are attempting, it may tackle a project mainly in order to outshine its rivals. In this case it will be tempted to plan a bigger project than it really needs, and one that will strain its resources too much. The bigger the scheme, the greater the community's prestige.

This was why some villages in the Udi division preferred to build their own feeder roads the whole way to the main road rather than link up with a neighbouring community's road-building project, and thus reduce the length of road they had to build. Others misdirected their efforts on buildings larger than they needed. Thus, while inter-village rivalry can provide a very useful stimulus, it must be used with care. The *main* stimulus must always be the people's wish to satisfy a local want. Excess of rivalry breeds wasteful and pretentious projects. It leads people into starting projects they may never finish, or do not maintain even if they finish them. It can also hinder neighbouring communities from jointly undertaking projects too large for any one community to undertake, such as, for example, building and maintaining one good senior school to serve them all.

All this means that the community worker must make sure that he is not stimulating communities to attempt projects mainly for reasons of prestige, but to meet a real and permanent need. He can also help in other ways to make each project a satisfying, educative, and encouraging experience for the people concerned.

Excellent work of this kind has been done in the Ahoada Division which, like Udi, is in the Eastern Region of Nigeria. The officer concerned had been in the division for several years and was well known and trusted by the people.

He made a practice always of arranging to meet people who wished to attempt a project, and he met them in their own village. He asked for a full village meeting so that before the project was started it could be thoroughly discussed by everyone, and not merely by a group of enthusiastic, self-appointed 'leaders'. At the meeting he stressed that everyone should help to decide on the form the project should take—women as well as men, illiterates as well as literates, commoners as well as chiefs and elders, newcomers to the community as well as those who had lived there all their lives. He pointed out that the more people there were who felt that they had had a share in deciding what should be done, the more people there would be who would willingly help by giving money or labour.

Secondly, he listened to the proposals for the project, and then by careful questioning helped the people to work out how much money and labour they would have to find and how they could provide it. He offered to provide plans, quantity specifications, and costings for the suggested project so that the people could choose what they would give to contract and what they could do by their own labour. He asked questions about how the completed project would be maintained, and if he found that the people expected the local government to maintain it, he suggested that they should ask in order to make sure that the local government would. He reminded them that the maintenance of projects costs money. Were they willing to pay a higher local rate if that should prove to be necessary? He also reminded the people to get in touch as soon as possible with any government officers whose permission or help they might need, and he offered to make any needed preliminary contacts for them himself.

Thirdly, he refused to consider requests for direct, material aid until the people could show that they had already done all they could for themselves. At that stage he would give some help, preferably by enabling the people to get roofing material and cement at 'wholesale' prices rather than by making them an outright gift of money.

Lastly, he left all *decisions* to be made by the people themselves at later meetings.

These methods have proved so successful that during the past few years Ahoada has been transformed from a relatively backward area with very poor communications into a division with a network of excellent roads linking up formerly isolated villages. Many villages now have their own communally built dispensaries, maternity homes, village halls, and schools, and some have excellent lorry parks as well. But in spite of their success these methods are still not generally applied throughout Nigeria. The trouble is that to work in this way is time-consuming, and time is a scarce commodity for government administrative officers in Nigeria today. It is much easier, and much quicker, for officers to stimulate 'development' by making grants from whatever government funds are available. Such grants, however, are no substitute for a skilful and sympathetic officer's time. They encourage a type of community mendicancy —an undue waiting on material help offered from outside the community—which may actually destroy the valuable self-help characteristic of this form of community development. The most important function of the government officer is to help communities to sort out their projects in the form which is most relevant to their needs and resources, and hence in the form that will give them most satisfaction when they are completed. This is essentially an educative process, and time rather than money is needed for it.

The government officer must not only be prepared to give his time, but also to give it at the right time of the year. People are much busier on their farms at some seasons than at others, and they can take on project work most successfully in the slack season when they have most leisure time. The project which is stimulated too late, so that it is left half-done when the busy season comes round again, may never be completed, and may prejudice the people against attempting other projects in the future. In the cocoa-growing areas of Ghana many people seasonally leave their villages to work on distant farms. In such areas the correct timing of project work is particularly important.

Most communities attempting projects expect the agency to give them some tangible, material help, however small, to supplement the efforts they are making for themselves. This help may take the form of a loan of tools, or of a skilled mason or carpenter, or it may be a gift of cement or roofing materials. Whatever form the help may take, if it is not forthcoming when the people are ready for it and really need it, they will feel that the agency worker has let them down, their enthusiasm will cool, and it will be hard for the worker to ekindle it. It is for this reason that the worker has to be careful not to stimulate more projects than he can service properly out of his available resources. For the same reason the agencies need to find ways of making the resources at their disposal immediately available when they are required, and not after a delay of several months. The aim must always be to supply some help, however small, at the time when it is most needed by the people.

One way of achieving this aim in the British African territories has been for the government to allow district officers to make grants from special funds allocated for the purpose. The grants were small, but they could be made quickly. But in some territories, e.g. Ghana, the development of local government to take over most of the former functions of the district officer, and the great increase in the size of the funds available for distribution in many areas, have made the system of allocating grants far more cumbersome than in the past. When the power of allocation is vested in the District Council, estimates of expenditure may have to be prepared and submitted, and applicants for grants may have to wait for a meeting of a local government committee. It has been noted in Ghana that:

There were many occasions when money to assist the villagers in their self-chosen projects arrived so long after

I. VILLAGE IMPROVEMENT
The village street before and after the community got to work

II. A PROJECT THAT FAILED (*see page* 52)

Above. Where the people tired.   *Below.* This they failed to maintain

application had been made through the usual estimates procedure, that the people had lost interest and were no longer willing to provide the labour they had originally offered.[4]

To provide aid when it is wanted is not solely, or even mainly, a matter of providing money. What the villagers really want are materials or skilled help of a kind not locally available. Thus the Burmese mass education department has very successfully created an enthusiasm for self-help in many villages, only, in some cases, to frustrate it. At Htaukkyant, near Rangoon, the people were anxious to rebuild their ramshackle bazaar, and urgently needed materials in order to get the work done before the coming of the rains. For these materials they were willing to pay, but the mass education officers, though sympathetic, could promise nothing. The people's request would have to take its turn through the usual government channels. At another village near Pegu the people needed skilled help with an artesian well, but no engineers were available to help them.[5] The same principle applies also to agricultural or health extension work. In Ghana a well-run campaign to get farmers to spray their cocoa trees against the swollen shoot disease was so successful that the supply of sprayers was quite inadequate. 'Our problem will be, in fact is, to keep the newly aroused interest of the cocoa farmers alive until sufficient quantities of sprayers arrive.'[6] In Nigeria, the showing of a film on smallpox brought many of the crowd forward to be vaccinated, but no one had thought of arranging for vaccinators to be present. It is this kind of situation that the project worker tries to avoid.

Village needs for specialist help on project work must normally be met from outside the community, but there are some occasions when the need for a particular skill is more permanent, and when it can best be met by some people in the community learning the skill themselves. It was partly with this kind of situation in mind that the Northern Rhodesian Government established an Area School in each of its special development areas. One function of these schools is to give village people elementary practical instruction in crafts so that they can do more than in the past to help themselves. [7]

The Ford Foundation has diagnosed a similar need in India. It has found that it is not enough for development to take place, or that people should want better tools or better houses. Such wants can only be permanently satisfied when there are blacksmiths, carpenters, and house builders in the village who are skilled enough to make, or at least to repair and keep in good order, the new kinds of tools and the improved types of houses. It is for this reason that the Ford Foundation has established as part of its Indian programme twenty training centres to provide special one-year courses of instruction for several kinds of village craftsmen. [8] Ellery Foster makes the same point when he argues the importance of establishing what he calls 'folk schools of next-steps technology' to provide special courses of instruction intimately related to village development needs. [9]

Most people think of community project work solely as a means of encouraging some local material development, such as a road, a clean water-supply, or the building of a school or maternity centre. Most projects do, indeed, take some such form, but there can also be projects with cultural, rather than economic and material objectives, and this is well illustrated by what happened among the Maori in the Auckland Province of New Zealand.

The Maori, like many other peoples affected by western influences, live in two worlds, for they retain much of their Maori culture. They have their own traditions, history, and oral literature. They have their own social structure based on kinship and supported by the many tribal functions that still take place. But at the same time they are

required to conform to the ordinary health standards, the ordinary educational standards, and the universal demands of economic well-being. In other words the Maori today lives in two worlds. He uses two languages and he often confuses the values in the separate systems. [10]

Economic progress is a part, but only a part of the Maori's total need. For many Maori it is as important to reconstruct the worthwhile things in their own culture as it is to produce more wealth.

M. Winiata, himself a Maori and a rural adult education extension worker, has written a very interesting article defining and illustrating what a community development agency can do in a situation of this kind. It is worth giving one of his illustrations at some length. It is a case of a community feeling after 'the vaguely known social memory of the group' because it wished to strengthen tribal life as a means of establishing and reinforcing its self-respect. Becoming aware of this situation and wishing to help, the agency sought out an elder of high status who had much of the required knowledge, and helped to disseminate his knowledge among interested members of the community.

Fortunately, this tribe had been thinking of renewing its meeting-house and having it carved as in olden times. The lack of experts in the craft anywhere near, the difficulty of getting tools for carving and the problems of obtaining the required type of timber were all obstacles. However, the facilities of Adult Education were brought to bear upon the situation and all these problems were solved. The Adult Education Office became a clearing house for the information needed, a specialist was engaged and financial arrangements were made between the local people and Adult Education which brought about a satisfactory co-operation. The young men of the tribe were formed into a carving school, the young women into the women's craft guilds required for decorating the interior of the building, while another group continued the study of the tribal history to use as bases for designs in the new building. At the end the whole community was in action on what was a communal project in a matter very significant to the tribe. The visits of the instructors became gathering days for the group as a whole. Some prepared food for the workers, others held dances to secure the finance for the project, all under the leadership of the local people with the encouragement of Adult Education.

Winiata gives other examples and he states the general principles on which the work of his agency is based, as follows:

i. to recognize that the people are a tribe and have leaders with definite status and functions;
ii. to recognize that the tribe has traditional ways of grouping people together for its own purposes;
iii. to start from the needs and interests of specific communities;
iv. to stimulate the people in each community to act under their own leaders, with the agency serving and helping rather than directing;
v. to work with the people rather than over them;
vi. to encourage people to educate themselves by doing.

These are sound principles for agency work in strong and active communities where people are accustomed to thinking and working together, and are already so conscious of what they want that they need only a little help and encouragement to spur them to action. But very many communities are not of this kind. In some, the people are divided by quarrels between factions and cannot easily agree to work together in their own common interest. In others, they feel so threatened by changes they do not understand that they have become ultra-conservative, determined to hold on at all costs to the known way of life which has given them security in the past and which they blindly hope will somehow continue to do so in the future.[11] It is significant that government community development agencies in West Africa have usually bypassed such 'difficult' communities in favour of more co-operative communities.

It is easy to justify such a policy in West Africa and in other areas where community development work has only recently been organized on a large scale, for it speeds up development by concentrating workers in those localities where they can obtain quick results. But it cannot be permanently justified, for by bypassing the difficult communities the worker thereby bypasses the communities that need help most. Sooner or later, therefore, the agencies have to tackle them. Methods of working in such communities are the subject of the next chapter.

CHAPTER VII

PROJECTS IN DISORGANIZED
COMMUNITIES

THE project worker in the apathetic or disorganized community has a much harder task than in the well-organized, traditional communities so far discussed. The people are not ready for projects, and he has to prepare the ground for them.

Many communities of this type are divided by factions, which make the worker's task more difficult. Leaders whom he thinks are village leaders may really be leaders only of a village faction. Even the official headman may represent a faction rather than the whole village, and by working mainly through him the worker may antagonize the other factions. Such factions may be based on kin, on religion, or on economic status, and the worker must get to know them and their leaders in order to avoid becoming too much identified with any one of them. He has to try to work with all of them, and to develop among them all a greater interest in the welfare of the whole community.*

It is with this kind of community development work that the Puerto Rican Division of Community Education is especially concerned. It is avowedly more interested in people than in targets; more interested in the

* For a stimulating study of village factions in relation to community project work, see Oscar Lewis, *Group Dynamics in a North-Indian Village*, published for the Programme Evaluation Organization, Planning Commission, Delhi, 1954.

process of development than in the material product; and as interested in working in depressed and difficult communities as in communities which readily take to new ideas.

This agency works in two stages. During the introductory 'extensive' stage the worker tries to get to know the people and win their interest and confidence. He visits each home in the many communities in his area, chats with the people, and asks them to join him in a group to study and distribute the educational books that he will bring. Every three months he arranges an early evening showing of educational films in an open-air gathering of the whole community.

The intensive stage follows whenever some of the people invite him to help them solve some local problem, but he still works slowly and cautiously:

He never pushes people into a reaction; he never himself states in a declarative way what he believes should be done; he does not try through words to mould opinion or to have the people come to a decision he himself may consider sound.[1]

He insists that everyone, rich or poor, landowner or worker, leader or follower, has the right to share in the discussions and to help make decisions; he urges that discussions should go on until all are agreed and that it is better to avoid an early decision by a majority vote; and he tries to delay the taking of specific action until the whole community is ready for it. He listens, starts discussions, waits till he is asked to help, and then helps by helping people to explore their problem.

This method makes for slow and seemingly formless work. Months of talking go past with nothing visible to show. We are told that one community spent nine months discussing the building of a school-house which it then completed in sixty days; that another talked for six months before it built a bridge; and that another took a year to move from asking the authorities to build a milk station to the opinion, stated at a community meeting amid applause, that this was a matter 'we ourselves must solve'. We are told that nothing can be done without interminable discussion.

It is the theory of the Puerto Rican agency that these 'interminable' months are not a waste of time, but rather the very web and texture of community development. It is during these months, so the agency believes, that the people gradually move out of their old patterns of thought and custom, achieve better understanding of their neighbours, investigate their needs and opportunities, and orientate themselves to change. These things take time, and it is the worker's main task to see that ample time is given. He has to discourage the zealous few from acting on their own. He has to try to draw everyone in to the process of choosing, planning, and doing. He has to delay action while the people develop friendship and confidence among themselves, and a feeling of solidarity that binds them into a community. The school, the bridge, the milk station, or the road is merely a material product that comes at the end of the process of community development and is subsidiary to it. 'The goal is not so much to accomplish or realize communal projects which will improve the living conditions of the people, but to help them to learn a way of living and working together which they may apply at any time to any problems which affect their communal life.'

For many generations the people have depended almost completely on government action for any improvement in their situation. The Puerto Rican agency aims to change this in a matter of months by promoting a thorough process of 'democratic group action'. By this means, it is claimed, people learn to solve their problems of communal living on 'a sound and permanent basis'.

It is very difficult to assess results in this kind of work. It is hard to measure change of attitude, and harder still to be sure that the change is permanent. To some extent, therefore, the Puerto Rican agency works on faith—a faith it hopes that time will justify. Meanwhile, it can show hundreds of completed projects, such as school buildings, roads, bridges, wells, and milk stations, which have been achieved in once difficult communities.

In the examples that have so far been discussed, the agency has always aimed at directly involving the *whole* community. This is a valuable kind of community development, but not the only one, and in practice it is subject to some very serious limitations.

The main trouble is that nearly everywhere there is only a restricted scope for projects of this kind, at any rate at present. In West Africa, for instance, roads and bridges, schools, markets, dispensaries, maternity centres, improved water-supplies, village halls and reading rooms, and, less frequently, co-operative shops and leper villages, make up almost the whole list of projects which have so far been attempted. True, to provide all or most of these and possibly to replan and rebuild parts of the village would seem to set any small community a formidable task, but the fact is that some villages have now provided themselves with all of these things that they need, or feel they need. Thus some formerly active villages have been quiescent for several years, and others may be expected to reach the same stage soon. The fact must be faced that however immediately rewarding this type of work may be, it is essentially sporadic and short-term in character, and so also is the *ad hoc* village committee which organizes the village for a project. Such committees often die when the project is completed.

Thus agencies which aim at starting a continuing process of development must soon look beyond the *ad hoc* village committee and the whole community project. They must widen their field by working with sectional and special interest groups within the community as well as with the community as a whole.

Such a policy may not always commend itself to people who think of community development essentially as a process by which the whole community strengthens and improves itself by common work for the common good. And, indeed, agencies must guard against promoting exclusiveness and conflict between community groups.* But for an agency not to work with special interest groups means that it is neglecting a whole range of fruitful and rewarding work. People act together when they share an interest or have a want in common, but not all wants and interests are equally felt throughout the whole community. It has been noted in Eastern Nigeria that the size of the 'community' tends to vary with the project: that while a whole village will turn out to labour on a road which is seen to benefit everyone, the cleaning of a water-supply that serves only a part of the village will be done by the villagers who will benefit most, with only token help from the rest.² While some special interests are thus based on neighbourhood, others are based on occupation or

* See pp. 33-4.

status within the community. These may be equally worthy of help, and by giving it the agency will also be stimulating and helping the community as a whole.

One of the best-known examples of community development work along these lines is the Antigonish Movement in the Maritime Provinces of Canada. This Movement was sponsored by the small Nova Scotian University of St. Francis Xavier. The Director, Dr. Coady, had the idea that extension education should be practical and down to earth, and he was particularly impressed by the possibilities of group action in the economic field. He aimed at helping people to acquire the knowledge and techniques they needed to solve their own local economic problems, and he aimed to help them in groups rather than individually. In groups, he believed, people would be more ready to work for the good of one another and of the community. He stressed two things: study to find out what needed doing most; organization through which what needed doing could be achieved.

His first approach was usually to people who had had some formal schooling and seemed to have ability as leaders, and he challenged them to do something 'about the desolation and poverty' around them. Then he got them to call a general meeting of the community, or to hold a number of small, informal meetings of neighbours in their homes. At these meetings Dr. Coady or one of his assistants would give a 'fiery and dynamic' speech, designed to stir the people up to do something for themselves. From the people who responded were formed the small study and discussion clubs which constitute the key educational technique in the Antigonish Movement. The Extension Department helped these clubs in many ways. It provided them with study materials. It arranged special training courses for their leaders. And it developed courses on community and co-operative organization to teach the leaders how to organize their groups for action. Later on, with the development of broadcasting, the Department broadcast wireless programmes to stimulate the clubs to discuss vital topics of local interest.

The people who joined the study clubs of the Antigonish Movement were mainly interested in learning how to work together to help themselves. Hence the most obvious result of this Movement has been a widespread development of co-operative societies of many kinds. Most of these societies are quite small, and they cater mostly for the particular needs of sections of the community rather than for the community as a whole. Thus there are co-operatives for fishermen and for farmers, co-operative house-building groups, credit unions, consumers' co-operatives, and insurance co-operatives.

These societies have greatly improved the economic situation of many of the people. Thus we are told of Morell, a typical farming and fishing community of about 300 families on Prince Edward Island. During the last fifteen years these people have achieved

... a new, large modern country store with an egg-grading station attached; in the same building, the credit union office; near by, a new lobster-canning factory, a frost-proof potato warehouse which holds fifty cars of potatoes, and a modern creamery with cold storage facilities; a community hall, with motion picture equipment and bowling alleys, and an outdoor skating rink providé recreation for young and old. The community has about $60,000 savings in its credit union. Through their co-operative store they are providing other services for the community: car repairs, tractor services for farmers, painting, installation of plumbing and electrical appliances. As problems arise, the people solve them for themselves.[3]

Improvements of another kind are also claimed, for it is said that these co-operative enterprises have developed a sense of realism and responsibility among the people, created really effective local leaders, and greatly improved relationships within many communities. Thus we are told that whereas in 1938 the people of Morell were divided on religious lines, the effect of co-operative development has been to promote a new spirit of neighbourliness. Religious intolerance has been outgrown. Relations between communities are also said to have improved. Local study clubs meet occasionally with those of near-by communities, and people begin to recognize that other people's problems are much like their own. Thus a feeling of inter-community goodwill is generated. In short, the Antigonish Movement has not only promoted rural economic development in a very depressed area; it has also developed a feeling of 'community'.

It is hard to size up this Movement from what has been written about it, and to learn from it all it has to teach. We are told of difficulties: of apathy and pessimism; of pride among the people so that even in desperate circumstances they will not admit that they need help. We are told, too, that many people resented the Movement's workers telling them 'how to farm or fish when we've been doing it all our lives'. And we are told that local leaders have sometimes been dishonest or incompetent. Such difficulties commonly face the community worker, but we are nowhere told how the Antigonish staff overcame them. Nor are we told enough about the balance between success and failure. The work has obviously been successful, but in how many communities, and to what degree? In how many has it been tried and failed, and for what reasons? These questions are important, but we are not told the answers. We are given only hints. We are told for instance:

If we had a thousand places like Morell in the Maritimes, we would have no Maritime problem.

But we are not told how many places like Morell there are, nor how far work in Morell was typical of work in other communities. In at least one respect it was not typical, for its study clubs were not started by the Movement's workers, but by two Morell students who 'had learned of the Antigonish theory of adult education' while studying at a university. What they learned stimulated them to work on the same lines in Morell, their home community.

Depressed and backward as the Maritimes were in the nineteen-thirties, it seems likely that the Antigonish extension workers had some advantages that similar workers in the tropics usually lack. The Maritime communities had once been prosperous. Their problem was to regain a prosperity they once had known, and depressed as they now were they were still part of a prosperous and progressive country and less isolated from the outside world than most tropical communities are. One may believe, therefore, that it was easier to stimulate the people there than in the tropics, where people lack these psychological advantages. Moreover, although most of the people were poor, they were not as poor as the people in many tropical rural communities: and although many people were illiterate, or virtually illiterate, there were others who were better educated. Can the study-to-action group technique be successfully used in tropical communities which lack these advantages?

One outstandingly successful example of this kind is provided by Jamaica's 'Better Village Plan'. As in the Maritimes there is a great emphasis on small group study, organization, and action, but there is a much greater emphasis than in the Antigonish Movement on linking up with existing community organizations, such as the church, parent-teacher associations, social clubs, branches of the Jamaica Agricultural Society, and co-operative and friendly societies. In addition, new groups are encouraged to form: co-operatives; Pioneer Clubs for the humbler people who do not already belong to any of the existing organizations; and youth groups of various kinds, including 4-H Clubs. All the groups are stimulated and serviced by trained organizers who help and encourage them to plan programmes which are interesting to their members and which include useful practical projects. New groups are visited by an organizer every few weeks until they have become well established.

To this aim of stimulating and multiplying active community groups the 'Better Village Plan' adds the further aims of founding a village committee of representatives of the groups, and of strengthening this committee until it can assume full status as a Community Council able to co-ordinate and supplement the activities of the various groups. Village committees and community councils are encouraged to organize joint activities, such as social hours and entertainments, at which the members of different groups meet and develop a friendly feeling.

The community council in Jamaica serves many purposes. It brings representatives of village groups together to study and discuss matters of concern to the whole village. It stimulates its member groups to action and puts them in touch with outside help when they require it. And it helps to unite the community for work on projects, such as the building of a road or village hall, which are too large for any single group to tackle on its own.

The development of the Better Village Approach was greatly influenced from outside Jamaica. One influence was C. F. Strickland's book, *Co-operation for Africa*. Another was L. F. Brayne's *Better Villages*, which described rural reconstruction work in the Punjab, and linked work on self-help and co-operative lines with the development of social organization through district community councils. A third was the example provided by the Antigonish Movement. In Jamaica as in the Maritimes the study club method is especially associated with the development of co-operatives. The fully-fledged co-operative society is registered only after its members have spent a year or more in study, saving, and work at some kind of co-operative project. Each group of ten or twelve members meets weekly to study co-operative techniques and to investigate how to apply them to the particular problems of the members of the group. Every member acts in turn as discussion leader and as secretary. The meetings also provide members with opportunities for singing, games, and dancing.

The stress on study is kept up even after the society has been registered. 'A regular program of education is carried out by societies for the benefit of members and Study Group sessions are held for new members.'[4]

Jamaica Welfare (1943) Ltd. was responsible for the

III. JAMAICA

Above. Community Centre at Guy's Hill, Jamaica (*see page* 85)
Below. The house on the right was built under a co-operative
housing scheme

IV. AT WORK IN THE VILLAGE

Above. A Jamaican 3-F Campaign demonstration (*see page* 73)
Below. Teaching village bandsmen in Ghana

development of this Better Village policy until 1949, when its work was taken over by the Jamaica Social Welfare Commission. By stimulating old and new groups in the rural communities of the island, it had helped people to satisfy many of their immediate needs, either by working on group projects or by joining savings unions, buying clubs, and co-operatives of other kinds. In 1945 this policy was enlarged to include a long-term mass education campaign which is known as the 3-F (Food for Family Fitness) Campaign.

This campaign presented Jamaica Welfare and its successor, the Jamaica Social Welfare Commission, with a task of a more difficult kind. The people were not as interested in the objectives of the new campaign as they were in their own group projects. 'People had to be made conscious of them through a process involving publicity, training, and group action', directed not only at the groups, but at every individual and family in the whole community.[5]

This led to a great emphasis on the training of leaders, and the concept of leadership was soon broadened to include anyone who showed initiative, who could teach something, or who was willing to learn. Such people have been regularly assembled for Get-Togethers and Zone Training Days and taken on outings to see successful ventures in other communities. Training days and training classes are also held in the leaders' own villages, and opportunities are provided for them to come together at residential camps. The training is designed to give the leaders ideas about the things that village groups can do and to show them how they can be done. The leaders are also taught how to preside at meetings, how to promote discussion, and how to organize projects. The headquarters provide staff and graded lists of suitable projects, together with simple explanatory literature, and they organize Achievement Days in connexion with the 3-F campaign and other community activities. These are community festivals at which the different groups feature displays of their work and receive awards. Competitions and entertainments are organized, and visitors are welcomed from all over the island. At these festivals learning is combined with enjoyment.

The Jamaica programme in its present form is the outcome of experiment since 1939, and it represents a relatively advanced and many-sided approach to community development work. It makes the utmost possible use of the project method. It stimulates group projects and individual projects (i.e. individual members are encouraged to practise at home what they learn at group meetings), as well as projects for the whole community. It develops a *permanent* organization within the community by helping groups to grow and by associating them on community committees or councils. It provides a specially trained staff to stimulate and service such groups and councils and to put them in touch with specialist, technical help if they should need it. It educates the groups in the techniques of democratic group action. It helps them to find out what they want to do and how to do it, and it encourages study by linking it directly to the will to learn. Nor is it content to work with the very limited number of acknowledged community leaders. Rather it aims at creating a capacity for leadership in every group member.

Rural development work in Jamaica has other noteworthy characteristics. Group and community representatives are encouraged to meet together both on an area basis and on the basis of special interests. Thus community councils are represented on district councils, and district councils on an all-island Welfare Association.[6] Farmers' and 4-H groups are linked by common membership of the Jamaica Agricultural Society. Co-operative groups are members of the Jamaica Co-operative Union or the Jamaica Credit Union League.

The different development agencies have also established a good working relationship among themselves. Both government and voluntary agencies are effectively represented on the Jamaica Social Welfare Commission: and this is reflected in the districts by close co-operation between the district officers of the Commission, the staffs of the Agricultural Department and the Jamaica Agricultural Society, the officers of the Education and Medical Departments, and the representatives of such bodies as the Women's Federation and the Central Council of Voluntary Social Services.

In spite of all this Jamaica does not entirely escape from the dilemma that faces nearly every rural development agency. Today, it is widely accepted that the ideal method of working is to stimulate people in groups and to help them organize their own development, rather than direct it for them. Compared with other methods this method is cheaper, more immediately effective, and more productive of permanent results. But it provides no simple solution to every problem of development. For project work to be really effective the people must adopt the project as their own. But what can be done when the people cannot, or will not, see their needs as the agency sees them? The Jamaican answer is reflected in the 3-F and the Home Improvement campaigns. These are still agency programmes rather than the people's programmes, and agency workers have to try to 'sell' them to the people and press them to tackle the projects that the agency desires. Thus in the plan of work for one district we read:

Projects

1. *Insist* [my italics] on every group carrying some one or more projects, with members undertaking individual projects as well.

2. Every group should at least participate in a community project.

3. Projects should run on the target system with the keeping of proper and accurate records and should be carried through to completion.[7]

Here we have more than a hint that people may be uninterested in the programme and need constant pressure to keep them up to the mark. When this is the case, most of the value of the project work is lost and the agency worker has to spend too much of his time 'checking on projects' and trying to 'revitalize' his groups.

What can agencies do when faced with this problem? It would seem that they can usefully do four things: check and reassess their programmes with a view to bringing them more closely into line with the needs the people feel; check the pace at which they are trying to introduce change, for perhaps it is too fast; check on the educational methods they use, for perhaps they can be made more effective; and, lastly, check on the kind of relationship their workers have established with the people.

There is always a real danger that the agency programme developed at headquarters may be out of touch with local circumstances; that it may reflect too much the middle-class values of its professional staff and too little the values and the economic circumstances of the people. Hadley has written a long article discussing the general effect of policies of this kind in the West Indies:[8] and Marier provides a specific example in the campaign against concubinage (customary marriage) sponsored by the Women's Federation of Jamaica.[9] It failed mainly because the women associated legal marriage with a standard of living most men could not afford.

It is equally important for the agency that wants to work with people rather than against them to watch the pace at which it tries to stimulate change. It is so fatally easy for the agency worker to become so preoccupied with the *need* for change that he pays too little heed to what he is demanding of the people. The really remarkable characteristic of rural development work in the tropics is not what is so frequently emphasized, that so many communities are apathetic and do not co-operate, but that so many so willingly co-operate so much. However co-operative people are and however good the cause, it may be asking too much to try to spur them on too often to undertake time-consuming project work, except in times of obvious crisis. It is sometimes overlooked that the ordinary community wakes up but rarely. What really matters is the quality of the day-to-day life of the community which must be protected from outside exploitation for outside purposes, though it must be able to respond to the outside world.[10] Maria Rogers, writing on this same theme, roundly condemns the attitude of the professional workers employed by welfare agencies (presumably she is referring to her own country, the United States of America): 'From the beginning', she says, 'these professionally trained "experts" have been a problem in local communities. Often they are not members of the communities in which they work. If they are, their professional training has successfully supplanted community norms and values by professional norms and values.' While 'serving' the local community they help to break it up. She describes them as 'community activists' and she notes that they have been responsible for a large variety of experimental projects in America. But she writes:

For the most part, in both rural and urban areas, such experimental demonstrations were disheartening failures. As soon as money gave out and professional workers departed, activities ceased.[11]

The 'community activist' approach is not entirely unknown in the tropics. The worker must often keep his natural desire for quick results in check if real involvement leading to permanent development is wanted.

To some extent the agency may be able to extricate itself from this dilemma by improving and perfecting its workers' educational techniques so that people more quickly recognize their needs as 'wants' demanding action. These techniques will be discussed in Chapters Eleven and Twelve.

However, it is not enough that the agency should develop 'a people's programme', work at the right speed, and make an intelligent and skilful use of educational methods. The agency workers must also establish a good relationship with the people they aim to serve. Lack of sympathy, tact, and understanding, the preoccupation of the worker with his own aims so that he fails to *feel* with the people, will prejudice even an admirable programme. This raises major issues of principle and method in the selection and training of agency workers which will be discussed in Chapter Thirteen.

In this chapter and in Chapter Six we have seen project work serving mainly material development, but we have noted that it may also lead to the development or strengthening of the people's feeling of 'community'. To the agencies mainly concerned with material progress, the moral stimulus of the project is merely a welcome by-product, as it were, of their work, but in the case of other agencies it may be the major aim, as it is in Puerto Rico. Community development of this kind is the main subject of the next chapter.

CHAPTER VIII

BUILDING COMMUNITY

IN all the examples we have discussed so far we have seen community development always as a process of developing a community which exists already. We now need to consider what the development agency can do where no community exists to be developed.

Such areas of 'no-community' have been created all over the world wherever rapid economic development and especially rapid industrial development, have occurred. People leave their own communities and come to them in search of work. They usually come as individuals, rarely as whole families, and still more rarely as members of some larger social group.

Most people leave community life to migrate into such areas in order to improve their material status.

Most of them succeed, but for a time they have to pay a social price. In rural neighbourhoods people are few enough for most of them to know each other fairly well. They have grown up together. They live and work in the same small place and realize that they have a common stake in it. They have a feeling of 'belonging'.

On migrating to a town, and especially to a large and quickly growing town, this feeling of belonging is lost. People live more of their lives apart. They come and go as individuals. They are more divided than united by their work. Initially, they have no common traditions, no common experiences, and no common standards of conduct developed by years of living in the same place. People can live in an urban neighbourhood for many years and hardly know their nearest neighbours.

And yet, of course, people in such places do often come together with other people at work, at church, at school, and in similar situations. They make friends and they join with other people to pursue together the interests they find they have in common. In these ways most people gradually manage to solve their own immediate social problems for themselves, though often on a narrow basis and usually without taking much interest in the places where they live. Others fail to adjust themselves and stay almost isolated from any kind of social life.

Faced with this kind of situation community agencies have to create rather than develop community, and most of them try to do it by attracting people into groups. Such groups may be for men, for women, or for youth: and they may appeal to special or to general interests. Most of them combine instruction with some social and recreational activities, and also with some measure, more or less limited, of self-government.

The process of community development (or creation) is envisaged in two stages: the first, development within the groups themselves as the members become more knowledgeable people, more friendly and co-operative among themselves, and more able to conduct their business without outside help and guidance; and the second, development in the community at large as the characteristics developed within the groups influence the conduct of the members in their homes and in their neighbourhood. Thus through the groups they sponsor, the agencies aim to produce socialized and community-minded people, as well as knowledgeable people. They may hope that leaders developed in their groups will later become leaders in community affairs. Moreover, they may hope to bring the groups themselves together on a Community Council or Association. As this finds common purposes and common targets, so the new community is born.

This in general is the broad, underlying theory on which much agency sponsoring of clubs and groups is based, but in most towns in the tropics work of this kind is still in its infancy, and agency resources are still woefully small. At the same time urban social problems are in many ways more acute and more difficult to solve than in the West. More people are really poor, and many of them are quite illiterate. Moreover, in many towns there are mixed populations of several races and tribes each with its own culture and its own language: while in some towns, particularly in Africa, there are many people who are only there for a few months or years before returning to their own village communities. On the whole, too, there is a much wider gulf than in the West between the agencies and the people they wish to help, and partly for this reason the agencies tend to leave less freedom to the groups they form. Thus on the Copperbelt of Northern Rhodesia, 'Rhokana Corporation insist that women wishing to attend their knitting classes should first attend classes on cookery and other homecraft subjects. Similarly no one can attend a dressmaking course until she has completed a handicraft course, at which wall bags, curtains, pillowcases, etc., are made by hand'.[1]

Unfortunately, the more the agency directs its groups, the less socially creative its work will tend to be. Most individuals are initially attracted to an agency group for what they can get out of it for themselves. At first they feel no responsibility for the welfare of their fellow members, or for the premises and property provided for them. Responsible attitudes, leadership, and initiative among the members develop only as real responsibility is given, and as the members come to feel that the group is *their* group serving *their* interests rather than an agency group serving agency interests.

This is the kind of statement that is easier to agree with than to heed in practice. All social agencies want to change things for the better, and in the tropics most of them are supported by public funds. They build their programmes for their groups on their own ideals of betterment, and they are able to attract people to these programmes. Too much freedom might well imperil the working of the programmes. Hence full freedom is withheld and people unattracted by the programmes stay away. 'Betterment' on agency terms is not for them.

But are agency programmes the sole criterion for community betterment? Some of us may judge the 'goodness' of a community by other standards, and the development of a community less as a process of

involving more and more people in agency-chosen programmes, than as a process of giving more and more
people more chances of joining more groups of the kind
they might wish to join: so that for more people their
neighbourhood becomes a more socially satisfying place
to live in. From this point of view agencies can be too
conscious of the importance of their own programmes,
and too little conscious of the importance of people
living a satisfying life. As Stephen Linton wrote
recently:

To ask what good youth clubs do is as unrewarding as to
ask what clubs in Pall Mall do: put that way the question
is invalid. [2]

This kind of question, one may think, is often equally
unrewarding in other fields of group and community
work. Even the organization of a group of young people
who met solely to enjoy boisterous games, and who were
not a bit interested in 'betterment' or in the further
education of themselves, contributed to community
development. For the young people who supported it,
and went on supporting it, it supplied something they
needed in their lives—something sociable and in complete contrast with the monotonous work at which they
spent their days—and we may think that it enriched community life as much for them as the 'more worthwhile'
youth and educational work promoted by the agencies
did for others. The real needs of the people may as
often be met by agencies descending to the people's
level, and helping them to do better what they want to
do, as by agencies trying to organize programmes of
their own.

Perhaps we can reach no fixed and general definition
of community development, and least of all of urban

community development. So much always depends on different local circumstances and different local and even individual needs. But if we must try, perhaps we can accept Allport's principle for improving human relations, and thereby developing community. He states it as follows:

Maximize situations in which the individual—child or adult—can participate fully and on terms of equal status in projects of joint concern to him and to his associates.[3]

And we may link to it Kelly's dictum that:

Teaching (including adult teaching) is primarily the business of making arrangements and affording a climate and conditions when growth may take place.[4]

On this basis the chief task of the community development agency is to help all kinds of democratic groups to grow, either by forming and sponsoring groups itself or by helping independent groups that people form themselves. In either case the emphasis is then on serving rather than directing the groups, and on helping them to develop contacts with each other, rather than on keeping them exclusive and apart.

Not every agency sees its problems in this light and though, as we have already seen, this is now the basic principle of the Jamaican 'Better Village Plan', it was not adopted till other methods had been tried and failed. The 'Better Village Plan' implies slow growth which the agency can help but cannot force. It recognizes that class and status differences, as well as differences of race and tribe and culture, tend to keep people apart and that people cannot be expected to bridge them easily. Where such differences exist the agency cannot develop a community merely by giving the people a community organization and a community centre in which to meet.

This is shown by the failure of the first approach Jamaica Welfare tried. It provided centres for two communities and installed a paid staff to arrange a varied programme of recreation and education. Members were allowed to elect their own management committees, but the paid staff remained responsible for the centres to Jamaica Welfare Ltd. which paid their salaries, and it was laid down that in the event of serious disagreement between the management committees and the staff, Jamaica Welfare should have the final say.

It was hoped that these centres would develop a local pride and community feeling by providing people with a common meeting place for games and recreation, and by stimulating and accommodating groups of many different kinds. Group projects were encouraged. Libraries and varied social and adult education programmes were provided. 'The emphasis was first of all on premises and facilities: when these were provided, it was believed, local leadership would emerge in many-sided activities.'[5]

Both centres failed after a few years. The warden of the Guy's Hill centre (1938–41) reported in 1940 that he was not getting the interest and support of members of his committee. The membership was never very large and many people joined solely to take advantage of the nursing facilities which were provided at the centre. They thought they should be entitled to everything free of all cost. They developed no leadership among themselves and they disagreed and quarrelled with one another. 'Imaginary social strata were a barrier to the best interests of communal development and brought about friction on many occasions.'[6] Yet 'imaginary' as the centre's workers thought these social strata were, they were apparently real enough to hinder community development and contribute to the failure of the centre.

The Jamaican experience is no isolated one, for the same approach was tried extensively in Tanganyika, Uganda, and Nyasaland, with the same result and for the same reasons. The centres failed to attract the common people and became, in fact, clubs for salary earners, with a Saturday night dance as the main attraction. It was difficult to collect even the smallest fixed subscription. Nowhere did a sustained interest in the centres develop. Nowhere did people make adequate use of the facilities provided.

Despite such failures and the lessons which they teach some agencies still rely on this 'community centre' approach to community development. Thus a community centre has recently been established in Koror, which is an American Trust Territory in the Palau group of islands in the Pacific. It has been given a full-time American director whose job it is to train Palauns to take over the direction of the centre. From the start it has been highly organized with many sub-committees. The aim is to stimulate sport and recreation of various kinds; to form interest groups; to develop educational activities; to start community projects to bring the age groups together; to train leaders from among the better educated people; and to develop local pride and community feeling. We are told that Koror is socially very disorganized; that rivalry and competition are rife, that there are many immigrants seeking jobs, and that there is no general feeling of community.* It will be very

* For a full account of the start of this experiment, see *The Koror Community Centre*, South Pacific Commission, Technical Paper No. 46, August, 1953.

interesting to study the course of this experiment during the next few years.

One reason why this kind of approach so often fails is that the centres are agency centres rather than community centres as long as their ultimate control remains with the agency. The people do not feel responsible for them. They can become *community* centres only when the people are ready to elect really representative and effective community councils to own them and control them. Thus the agencies face a dilemma. While agency control continues, the centre fails to develop community because the people do not feel responsible for the centre and resent the agency's control: yet until they have the community feeling which the centre is established to develop, they cannot effectively control the centre for themselves. The community centre approach to community development is all too often wrongly conceived. It should come after, not before, the people have developed a sense of community.

It is always worth remembering that the community is primarily a social group, and based on the *feeling* that people have for one another.[7] It can exist without formal organization and it is not ever necessary that people should be conscious of having the same aims and interests, though this may help. In essence, it is the feeling of belonging to, and sharing responsibility for, the welfare of the group. It grows by people meeting and liking each other in small and democratic groups of every kind, and learning to consider the welfare of other people and respect their opinions. As and when this feeling of 'belonging', and the social attitudes it teaches, are applied and extended outside the small group to the whole neighbourhood in which the people live, so the real community is born. It is the weakness of the directive agency that it retards the growth of the basic feeling of 'belonging' in the groups and institutions it creates.

Many agencies other than those which specifically do community work, contribute to community development by stimulating this basic feeling. Even the most formal type of adult education class will often show signs of rudimentary social growth. Its members go on outings together, or they may organize a dinner or a dance. But sometimes this social development will go much further. If the subject of study is in any way related to community affairs so that the students get interested in some local problem through discussion, an adult class will sometimes produce a self-formed group for social action. Some of the most active development groups and progressive societies in Ghana have originated in this way.

Similarly, a formal Evening Institute may become a real centre of social growth. For example, there is a Men's Institute in a working-class area in the East End of London. It has over 2,000 working-class students—dockers, carpenters, fitters, tailors, and factory hands, and it provides almost any class these people want. There are classes in shoe-repairing, furniture repairing, car maintenance, and making and repairing wireless sets. There are classes in pigeon, chicken, and rabbit rearing, in house decoration, and even in weight-lifting. And, of course, there are also classes in drama, painting, music, and other cultural subjects.

This Institute has no specific social policy. It aims to serve the people by providing them with rooms in which to learn, and with teachers to help them do whatever they may want to do. In all this it serves the people well, but the most interesting development is the clubs the people form. These are not in any way sponsored by the Institute. They are formed by the students because they are not content to meet only as learners. They form the clubs alongside the classes, for friendly talk and discussion of their hobbies. Thus they develop social bonds. Men will stay on in a class long after they have learnt all the teacher can teach them because they do not wish to lose their 'club'. The Institute has become much more than an adult school. It has become a centre for social development, not by organizing it, but by providing conditions which favour social growth.

There are lessons here for social development workers in the tropics in spite of the difference in environments. The key principles are to leave the people free, to consider their feelings and their needs, and to try to serve their *wants*. These principles are well illustrated by some recent developments in Dar-es-Salaam.

Dar-es-Salaam is the chief town in Tanganyika, and many illiterates have migrated to it in search of work. It was thought by the Government that experience of urban life must lead them to want to learn to read and write, but all attempts to attract them into classes at the government Welfare Centres had failed. Most of the illiterates live in urban settlements on the outskirts of the city and they will not stay at the Welfare Centres near the centre of the city once their working day is done. For this reason an adult literacy scheme was launched in 1952 with the idea of taking to the people where they lived the means of becoming literate.

These settlements, we are told, were without social cohesion:

In them, 'the homogeneous tribal village, where life was regulated by accepted standards of social and moral behaviour, and a common language, has given place to a heterogeneous mingling of African peoples, separated by tribal conservatism, prejudice and ignorance, and as yet not fabricated into an urban social entity'.[8]

By using posters ('The illiterate was shown bewildered before a signpost, confounded at a bus station, being thrown out of a "ladies", and at the mercy of a smooth pay clerk'), and by attracting the people by a mobile cinema to a meeting to discuss the formation of classes, in the end nine classes were formed. Government supplied blackboards, lamps, and honoraria for the part-time teachers, while the students paid for their reading and writing materials. Four months later, thirty-six out of the seventy people in the class at Kinondoni passed their literacy test, and their subsequent history is interesting.

So far the students in this group had met under a tree out of the public eye, but they were now proud of their success and were determined to learn English. They decided, entirely on their own, to build a school, and they proceeded to do so, making the furniture for it and decorating it, and in three weeks it was completed. Meanwhile, the Social Welfare Department was doing what it could to help and support their new-found sense of initiative.

The new school was made a listening point for the radio service being developed by the Social Development Department. The 'Graduation Ceremony' was recorded and broadcast on the news and the names of those successful in the literacy tests were announced on the radio. Photographs of the group, of the opening day, and of individuals were taken and prints sold at a subsidized rate to each member of the group, and the local press published a full page illustrated article on 'The Kinondoni Adult School'.[9]

The difficulty of providing this and other groups with teachers of English was partly overcome by the offer of voluntary work by members of the Dar-es-Salaam Rotary Club. At Kinondoni there were now thirty-six people in the English group and twenty-four still learning Kiswahili. Of these, fifty-seven were in the age-group eighteen to thirty, the remaining three being older. The group was composed of representatives of twenty-three tribes. Only four were local tribesmen.

But how is this adult school development related to community development? It appears to be related in several ways.

'During the year', we are told, 'three football clubs have been formed in Kinondoni. The Adult School has cleared a football ground, bought footballs and posts, and organized matches with the teams of other Adult Schools.

'In the past several attempts had been made by a very worthy voluntary organization to make provision for sewing classes for the Kinondoni women. There had been no response to appeals to the men to erect a temporary building for this purpose, and in fact materials supplied for this building disappeared from the site. Three months ago the members of the Adult School voluntarily agreed to allow the women to use their building, and now the women are studying Kiswahili and English. Delegations from other villages have come to Kinondoni to see the school and four of the schools now being built are of the Kinondoni pattern.'[10]

The adult school also organized an inter-village sports day with four of the other adult schools competing. 'This was a great day in the life of the village, with spear-throwing, jumping, and running', but still more important was the broadening of social life, and the changed attitudes of people towards each other.

The boys' club movement in Lagos and in the Western Region of Nigeria provides a quite different illustration of the same principles at work. Here the Social Welfare Department approached a few likely men and women in each urban neighbourhood to interest them in starting youth clubs. It is the way the clubs were started and managed that is interesting and significant. In each case a few local people were asked to contact one or more local boys, to discuss the idea of a club with them, and then to ask them to talk things over with their friends to see if they wanted a club, and if so what they wanted it for. After this, if it became clear that a club was desired, the *boys* were asked to find adult 'helpers' to act as leaders in the activities they wanted, and to find 'honorary members' to support their club financially. Thus, right from the start, and in a very real sense, responsibility for the club lay solidly with the boys. It was their own club, not an agency club provided for them.

The clubs started in this way are open clubs, unattached to any religious denomination or voluntary society. Their link is to the neighbourhood in which the members live and from which the helpers and honorary members mostly come. Because of this the clubs help to strengthen and promote local neighbourhood and community feeling, even in areas where it is weak. Through their clubs such neighbourhoods become more conscious of themselves. They follow the fortunes of their clubs in leagues and competitions with similar clubs and take pride in their successes. People feel that a good club reflects credit on its neighbourhood.

Here again the agency, the Social Welfare Department, does not aim to own and 'run' the clubs. It aims to help and serve them, not control them.

The non-directive agency in fact can work in many ways. It can do a lot to help small, independent groups to form and thrive. Sometimes their most important need is somewhere to meet, especially in new and growing towns where there are few halls and rooms available for meeting in. Large community centres are often too distant, and too grand, and have too few *small* rooms available to be able to meet this need properly. Again, the agency can serve such groups by putting them in touch with the kind of help and advice they want, as the Social Development Department did at Kinondoni, or it can help groups to gain status and recognition in their neighbourhood. The Men's Institute in London does this by staging public exhibitions of the work of students' clubs. In Trinidad, rather anti-social gangs of youths were brought closer to their communities when they were helped to improve their 'steel bands' and to represent their neighbourhood in steel band competitions.

While discussing agency work with groups we have always so far been considering groups of a formal kind, however friendly and informal the actual meetings of the groups may be. They are governed by rules, and they have chairmen, secretaries, treasurers, and committees. They have a recognized purpose, and need to be formally organized to carry it out. It is the purpose which attracts new members to the group.

Most community agencies are interested in this type of group, but people also form groups solely on the basis of congeniality. Such friendship and habit groups may have no defined purpose, no officers, and no rules. People form such groups solely because they like each other and enjoy each other's company. They are found in every type of culture and community. They exist in the tropics in the women who habitually chat together at the village well or water-hole, and in groups of men who meet in the evening under a village tree or at a particular table in the coffee shop. They exist in Western society in the small knot of men who habitually meet each other at the pub on Friday night, and in the groups of women who meet for tea in each other's houses.

Agencies usually neglect groups of this kind either because they are unaware of them, or because they cannot easily contact them, or because they do not recognize them as important. Yet they are *potentially* important. People learn most easily among friends. Many people will not take the risk of appearing ignorant among strangers and will only join an agency-sponsored group if they can persuade one or two friends to join with them. Others will not join such a group at all. They prefer to stay among their friends, and they give the agencies and their workers a wide berth. It is for this reason, says Maria Rogers, that the clientele of community agencies usually numbers, not members of the community's informal groups, 'but "isolates" and near-isolates, who have no close relationship with groups, are lonely most of the time, and looking for friends. This section of the community—a floating crowd of disassociated persons—receives the bulk of the ministrations of the welfare agencies and swells their attendance figures.'[11]

Some detailed studies of informal friendship groups have been made in the United States. Thus H. H. Doddy, investigating such groups among 100,000 people in Manhattanville, a depressed area in New York City, identified 218 entirely self-formed groups unknown to the community agencies. This, he says, has general implications for any type of community programme. He goes on:

It is axiomatic that a program of community improvement must involve as many people as possible to achieve its goals. When the program is concentrated on formally organized groups alone, at least half the total population will be excluded from participation. . . . Under these circumstances the efforts of institutional groups to improve the community are cancelled out by the apathy of the many informal groups who play no part in such efforts. They are at best indifferent, if not overtly hostile. [12]

He goes on to suggest that urban social agencies must become aware of the existence and importance of these groups, meet them on equal terms, establish friendly relationships with them, and try to get them more interested in their neighbourhoods. This would involve, he says, some change in the existing emphasis, which is to appeal to individuals to join an institutional programme on the basis of an individual interest, and which disregards the basic foundation of personality attraction which holds the informal group together. He concludes:

The adult educator must work in every way to improve the small (informal) groups in the community, to help them grow and mature, to urge them to accept more challenging tasks, to help them see relationships between their problems and those of other groups, and to help them recognize the advantage of co-operative efforts in solving community problems. [13]

This is easier said than done, for friendship groups are inconspicuous as well as numerous, and unlikely to welcome the attentions of the community worker. But some agencies have tried, and one of the more successful attempts is that of the Community Education Project of the San Bernadino Valley College in California.[14]

This project was started with the help of a subsidy from the Ford Foundation's Fund for Adult Education. The scheme was based on a series of weekly radio programmes, each lasting for half an hour, and designed to develop people's interest in public affairs. Themes were chosen, and each theme was dealt with in a series of nine programmes. Each programme was 'open-ended' and so presented as to stimulate discussion.

There was nothing new in this, for examples of the use of wireless programmes to stimulate discussion can be found in many countries. What was new was the kind of group—the informal friendship group—the project was designed to reach.

The project was run in close co-operation with a daily newspaper which publicized each programme, carried supplementary feature articles on the topic of each programme, and suggested questions for discussion.

At public meetings and through the Press, people were invited to get their friends together to listen to the programmes, and then discuss the issues they presented, choosing their own discussion leader for each meeting. To help the groups the agency held weekly meetings anybody could attend. At these meetings group members were helped to learn the techniques of discussion and to solve the difficulties experienced by the different groups from which they came.

It is claimed that this combination of radio, newspaper, and home discussion group has helped to revitalize community life. By April 1954, one year after the project had been started, over 100 friendship groups had taken part in it. 'Over the past eight months, several thousand men and women in the communities in the Valley have left whatever else they might have been doing on a Wednesday evening to get together with their friends to talk over these radio programmes.' Many of them, it is said, have thereby been stimulated to become more active members of their communities.

So far we have seen urban community development mainly as a matter of forming groups or of helping social groups to thrive, but it is commonly accepted that this should be followed by a second necessary and important stage—that of bringing groups together, enlarging their purpose, assisting them to define common targets for their neighbourhood, and encouraging them to work together to reach the targets. This usually involves creating a community council to organize the programme.

These are unexceptionable aims, and there are in fact many people who see urban community development solely in these terms. For them the hallmark of the good community is that the people in a neighbourhood should be willing to act together for the good of their community. According to this view the main job of the community development worker, or (significantly) community *organizer* is to stimulate and organize activities.

Unfortunately, it is easier to organize than to educate, easier to plan a programme of community betterment with a few people than with many, and easier to stimulate a few action groups in the community than to increase tolerance and respect for the opinions and feelings of other people. Thus many community workers measure their success mainly in numbers of groups and in the activity of groups. Changes in people's attitudes towards each other are harder to achieve and harder to measure.

Yet it is easy to overstress the value of community

activities and to underestimate the importance of good community *feeling*, especially if there is a danger of people being pressed into activities they do not really like for fear of being branded as unco-operative. P. H. Mann makes this point very cogently when he discusses the modern neighbourhood theory of town planning as it is applied in England.[15] He suggests that the basic principle for urban community development should be to ensure that as far as possible people are well adjusted to their neighbours and have a 'neighbourly' feeling towards them.

He argues that there are two kinds of neighbourliness—manifest and latent. Manifest neighbourliness he defines as active participation in social and community activities; latent neighbourliness as favourable attitudes between neighbours. Of these two kinds, latent neighbourliness is by far the most important, for without it social and community activities may degenerate into a hollow sham. There are two kinds of people: the manifestly sociable who like to visit and gossip with their neighbours and who are active members of the many groups they join; and the less overtly sociable who are more selective in their friendships, and who want to live their own lives in their own way, rather than in a crowd. These people are not therefore bad members of their communities: nor are the sociably minded people necessarily good. What really matters is that they should all have favourable attitudes towards each other which can result in positive action when a need arises in time of crisis or emergency. This is endangered by too much stress on getting the maximum possible number of people to participate actively in ordinary community life. Many people resent the resultant pressures, even if they unwillingly comply with them to some extent, and they develop less favourable attitudes towards their neighbours. The feeling of community is weakened although the outward form goes on, and the high degree of manifest neighbourliness can be mistakenly taken as proof of social solidarity. Conversely:

. . . if, at first visit, a neighbourhood appears to be sleepy and apathetic, with absolutely nothing happening at all, this is no reason for thinking that the inhabitants lack neighbourliness. If the observer can go below the surface to discover the latent neighbourliness, he may well find a very definite attitude expressive of social cohesion. In the modern urban neighbourhood this may well be the most important factor of all. [16]

CHAPTER IX

THE SCHOOL AND THE COMMUNITY

IN all the community development schemes and projects described in the previous chapters, the agencies have always needed in some way to instruct or educate the people in what to do, or in how to organize themselves, or in the skills they needed to reach their new objectives.

Since people ordinarily associate education with schools, and since nearly every small community in the tropics now has a school, or access to a school, it may therefore seem surprising that so far there has been no mention of the school as a means of educating communities. The truth is that except in a few areas the school has not so far been very effective in helping small communities to adapt themselves constructively to change. Indeed, it is sometimes argued that it has more often tended to cause them to disrupt.

To understand the reasons for this we must look back to the origins of the school in the tropics, and we find that it was originally a Western innovation introduced and controlled by missionaries or governments to serve their own ideas of what was good for people, rather than what the people thought was good. Indeed, the school was usually intended to supplant the indigenous forms of community education, and it introduced ideas and values which often directly conflicted with those already existing in the community. Thus the schools controlled by missions taught a Western form of religion, not the traditional religion of the community, and the secular curriculum in nearly every school was formal and bookish. Such curricula were designed primarily to instruct children in the knowledge and skills they needed to get jobs in the larger society outside their own community rather than to fit them better for life within it.

The school therefore was essentially a foreign institution with little direct relevance to community life.* While people remained unaffected by the economic and political pressures of the larger society they did not value it, as many of them still do not value it today. Difficulties in enrolling children to form new classes,

* See 'Special Study on Educational Conditions in Non-Self-Governing Territories', United Nations, 1954, pp. 70–1, or an extract, 'Community Development and the School' in *The Community Development Bulletin*, Vol. VI, No. 4, pp. 84–5.

poor attendance figures, and heavy 'wastage' of pupils leaving after only two or three years at school are all symptoms that the school is not valued in the community and that it is having only a negligible effect on community life.

In time, as people acquire one or more of the values of the external society to which the school belongs they may come to value the school as well. If they adopt Christianity, for instance, they may send their children to a mission school to be instructed in the faith, but of all the possible external values they may learn, most often it is the value of money and of individual, material, economic advantage. 'It is not taught them by the school, it is taught by almost every adult contact they may have with the outside world, but as they learn it, so they come to value the school in proportion to the teacher's ability to help their children to a good start in life.'[1] As opportunities for employment outside the community increase, and as people realize that the school is a gateway through which their sons must go if they are to get good jobs outside the community (and thus be able to support them better when they are old), so the school, the formal curriculum of the school, and the teacher, come to be valued as a means to individual advancement and escape from the existing poverty of community life. But they are still not valued as a means of adapting and developing the community from within.

At the same time the school and the teacher may be valued for yet another reason if, as sometimes happens, the people want a school in order to maintain their prestige with rival neighbouring communities. Here the school is prized less for its educational value than as a symbol of community status.

Such reasons provide quite enough incentive for

people to make considerable sacrifices to obtain a school for their own community, even if they have to build it for themselves. But this alone does not make the school effective in community education. Indeed, it may have the reverse effect, for the people have now found their own uses for the school as it is, and they may resist outside attempts to modify it and expand its now traditional functions.

Yet that is just what some governments and missions now want to do. They have realized that the school, as they had first introduced it, was encouraging 'an unregulated individualism which is destructive of the best elements of communal life', and that 'in so far as its influence tends to weaken social bonds, to undermine the traditions, affections, and restraints that unite men with one another and generation with generation and to introduce a new set of values entirely unrelated to the old, its effects are harmful rather than constructive'.[2]

These bad effects, they feel, could be avoided by linking the teaching in the school more closely to the life of the community. They now want children in school to be taught to understand their own local environment, to study the laws and customs of their tribe, and 'to make as large a use as possible of local folklore, stories, songs, arts and crafts; and to strengthen the loyalties and bonds of native society'.[3]

This desire to relate the school curriculum more closely to local community life in the hope of retarding community disintegration has been powerfully reinforced by the modern stress on community development, and many people now want to make the school a main agency, or even *the* main agency, for community education. The teacher must relate his teaching to the people's way of life in order to help them to improve it. He is seen as the ideal person through whom new ideas can reach the community.

This is an attractive idea. It is hard to find enough workers for community work in villages. The school teacher seems admirably to fill the gap. He is already in the village, he is paid and controlled by an outside agency, and he is a professional educator. If he is properly trained and supervised, may he not in fact become a key community worker?

A great deal of wishful thinking has grown up around this idea, but it has tended to overlook some of the real difficulties which must first be overcome. We have already noted one of them: that people now have fixed ideas about the nature and the value of the school, and may resist attempts to change it. Many people in the tropics firmly believe that the school teacher's job is to teach the children, and to teach them the school 'subjects' that have become traditional. They do not expect the teacher and the school to concern themselves directly with the affairs of the adult community, and they tend to react unfavourably when they do. In the Philippines, the teacher who took the children out of the classroom into the village to clean up the village square was resentfully told to stay in the classroom where she and her pupils belonged.[4] The reforming teacher needs to approach the community with tact and skill if he or she is to avoid becoming the subject of boycott and persecution.

The teacher, of course, has much more freedom of action within the school itself. He can try to make the curriculum more practical and more closely related to community life. For instance, he can teach and demonstrate better practices in health and hygiene, and ensure that children practise them in school. But it is another matter to get them carried over into the community. Adults are not ordinarily influenced much by children. It is a brave child who will persist in telling his mother that the way she runs her home is wrong, and a clever one who will convince her. Moreover, not all children will want to. They have grown up in the community, were under its influence before they went to school, and remain predominantly under its influence while they attend school. Under these circumstances the teacher trying to affect community behaviour through the children has to be very skilful to achieve his object. His main hope must always be that they will influence it as adults, *after* they have left school.

If this were all he could do the teacher would have to wait for years to see results. It is therefore argued that the teacher must act directly on the adult community, using all his tact and skill to overcome resistance to his new activities. But in spite of directives issued to teachers by their agencies the results in most territories have been disappointing. Teachers either have not tried, or they have tried and failed.

This is not surprising. It is quite unrealistic to expect the ordinary teacher in most rural areas in the tropics to become the leader and stimulator of the village in which he works. Successful community leaders are men of high community status in the sense that they are liked and trusted by their neighbours. Usually they have been born and bred in the community. They are no longer young. They know the community and are known by it. Some teachers satisfy these conditions, but most do not. They are usually strangers and responsible to an outside agency rather than to the community in which they work. They start unknown to the people.

They are often young and usually poorly paid. They may have become teachers only because they failed to qualify for more attractive work in towns. Thus they start with many disadvantages, and only a minority of teachers achieve such a high status where they teach that they become able to exert a strong influence in community affairs. Even if they do, they do not permanently reside in the community. They are always liable to be transferred elsewhere.

There is another limiting factor which is sometimes overlooked. The teacher who does try to become a community leader takes on a very heavy task. In school, he can no longer give formal lessons from the textbook. He must explore the neighbourhood, probe into its problems with his pupils, and base his own curriculum on what they find. For the poorly educated teacher this involves an immense and continuing effort even if he has been trained in how to make it, which often he has not. It means, too, the sacrifice of most of the leisure which he often feels is his main compensation for the low salary he is paid. Even so, much more is often expected of him than merely to reorganize his school curriculum. Thus he may be expected:

to organize the co-operative society in the village, to improve agriculture, to organize adult literacy campaigns, to run a night school, to dig latrines and pits for the village, to plan houses, to grow flowers, to pour oil on mosquito-infested ponds, and, incidentally, to teach his pupils four or five hours a day.[5]

In practice, most teachers have neither the time and energy, nor the status in the community, nor the requisite education and training, to undertake such activities successfully.

Before we go on to examine what has actually been done to promote community development through the school we must note a difficulty of another kind. Where there is only one school in a village it is possible to visualize that somehow or other it may in time become a true community school, and even a community centre, by serving and educating the whole community. But in many small communities there are at least two schools, each controlled by a different (religious) agency. In this situation neither school can claim to represent the whole community, and the schools serve the community best by working in harmony together. If they compete or conflict, they are more likely to hinder community development than to promote it.

A second difficulty arises when, in the interest of efficient instruction, several small village schools are closed in order to concentrate pupils in a larger school near by. However desirable and even necessary this may sometimes be, it does have one unfortunate effect, for it inevitably deprives several small communities of their own local school and of their own resident teacher. To the extent that the teacher may be expected to promote local community development, to that extent these communities are the poorer. They have lost a potential adult community centre in the school and a potential community leader in the teacher.*

In spite of all these real difficulties there have been many attempts to use the school as a centre for community education, notably in East Africa through the Jeanes teachers, and in Latin America and the

* For interesting short studies of some of the social effects of school reorganization policies, see W. C. Radford, 'Socialisation, the Large School and the Rural Child', *The Forum of Education*, Vol. VIII, No. 2, Teachers' College, Sydney, N.S.W., and *Community Service News*, Vol. XI, No. 4, 'Basic Issues in School Consolidation'.

Philippines. The Jeanes teacher was a visiting teacher specially trained to help village teachers to influence adults as well as children. He worked in close touch with other community workers concerned with health, agriculture, and home improvement, and specifically aimed to promote co-operation between school and community.

He was to promote community and home recreation; exhibitions, festivals, sports, and competitions; village libraries; co-operative marketing, trading, and saving; women's guilds; youth organizations; and community buildings.[6]

Unfortunately, the Jeanes teachers failed to win enough support among the village people and after some time the scheme was abandoned.

Mexico has also tried a variation of the same approach in its cultural mission programme, which was developed primarily for Mexico's tribal Indian communities. Each mission consisted of a number of specialists—in home economics, nursing and midwifery, agriculture, building and allied trades, and music and recreation. Its task was to try to ascertain the people's needs and then to stimulate and educate the people to satisfy them. At first these missions worked with and through the rural school, but this policy was abandoned in 1948.[7] Implicit both in this scheme and in the work of the Jeanes teachers is the recognition that in these areas the school teacher lacks the status, the ability, and the time to influence the adult community unaided.

The school also featured significantly in a project sponsored at Viani in Colombia, South America, by a local Institute of Anthropology and carried through by a field consultant sent there by Unesco.[8] The consultant found that the teachers' programmes were laid down for them by higher officials and that they took no interest in community affairs.

She developed a five-part programme designed to bring the school curriculum much more closely into line with local living conditions, and to carry its influence from the school into the community. Her first step was to encourage the teachers to pay regular visits to the homes of the children so that they could understand their home conditions and daily problems. The second was to use the understanding thus gained to reorientate the school curriculum so that much more time was given to the teaching of farming and gardening, personal health and hygiene, housekeeping, cooking, and the care of clothes. All these subjects were closely related to local conditions and were taught practically in the farm and garden, in the school kitchen, and in the classrooms. The children cleaned the schoolrooms, repaired the furniture, furnished and decorated a living room and a lunch room, organized the serving and clearing away of meals, and made play equipment out of old tyres, barrels, boards and rope. In all this the emphasis was on the children finding and adapting whatever resources were locally available.

The problem of getting some of this activity carried over into the homes was also tackled. As the children progressed through the various stages of the new curriculum they were asked to apply what they had learnt at home by means of a graduated series of 'home projects'. It was one of the duties of the teachers when they visited the children's homes to check up on the way these projects had been carried out.

The Unesco account of this project describes only five months' work, which is too short a time to provide a sound basis for evaluating its success. Even so, one difficulty was soon encountered. The key factor in this project was regular home visiting by the teachers. It was needed both to keep them continuously aware of community needs and to check on the home projects by which the teachings of the school were to be practically applied in the home. But although we are told that the teachers 'got highly interested in the work', we are also told that they found many homes distant from the school and difficult of access, since they were in the mountains; and that there was too little time for visiting between the close of school and the onset of darkness. One cannot but wonder whether home visiting persisted after the first enthusiasm had waned and the consultant had gone.

A somewhat similar scheme was developed over a much wider area in Guatemala. As in Colombia the new school curriculum centred around the three major fields of agriculture, health, and home life education, and big efforts were made to carry it over into the adult community. Two factors were felt to be specially important: the organization of close supervision by the relatively small group of trained teachers whose job it was to see that the untrained teachers did what they were expected to do; and the development of children's and parents' organizations through which the school extension programme could be taken into the community.[9]

The children's organizations are known as 1-G Clubs, the Guatemalan adaptation of the United States 4-H Club idea. The clubs work on a project system. 'These projects in some cases are group projects, designed to benefit the entire school or the entire community, as for example the school garden project, the water-supply project, or the latrine construction project. In other cases, the projects are carried on individually in the different homes of the club members. These projects include home improvement and home cleaning, sewing, home garden, chickens, rabbits, or pigs, and the construction of sanitary facilities in the home. In every case, the club member must apply what he has been taught in school in carrying out his project.' [10] It is emphasized, however, that although this programme has proved beneficial, it can never take the place of other agency programmes. It is merely 'an essential supplementary activity'.

Both the Colombian and Guatemalan schemes are essentially of the same kind as the directive schemes discussed in Chapter Five. The teacher or his supervisor decides on what changes are needed and tries to introduce them into the community through the school. It is difficult work and the knowledge, skill, and tact required for it are beyond the reach of very many rural school teachers, especially if they are young and lack community status. These are weaknesses which are not overcome by closely supervising the teachers, as in Guatemala, or by temporarily stimulating them and making things easier for them by introducing a highly qualified worker into the community for a short time, as in Viani. It must not be forgotten that the teacher, as a teacher, has plenty of work to do *in the school*. To make him also responsible for continuous extension work outside the school is usually to ask too much. Only the quite exceptional teacher will put his heart into it.

This difficulty is interestingly overcome in a scheme which was started in Kashmir in 1939. The schools were being reorganized in curriculum and teaching methods to bring them more into line with local community needs, and also with the object of developing more sympathy and understanding between school-educated people and their less well-educated neighbours. Out of this development came the idea of organizing an annual 'Labour Week' in all the State's primary and secondary schools.[11] The main purpose of this Week was the education of the school children in the social and moral values of working for the community. Thus unlike the projects already discussed it was not primarily aimed at the education of adults. It was, however, hoped that one result of the week would be to help students and adults alike to realize the identity of their interests and to relate the school more closely to community life.

Several factors seem to have contributed to the success of this project. From the first it was emphasized that success would depend above all on a careful planning of the work to be done after a survey of the means and resources available to each school. As far as humanly possible all the children were to be usefully and continuously employed all the time on projects suited to their powers. Secondly, the authority responsible for the schools took time and trouble to win the co-operation of the teachers, and through them of the children. The teachers were asked to help their students realize 'that they were participating in a significant and freely chosen activity of great social value'. The students themselves were asked to suggest the kinds of work that should be done both in and outside the school.

During the Week the normal school curriculum was entirely suspended and all kinds of projects were carried out instead. The schools, together with their furnishings and equipment, were cleaned and repaired; stones, glass, and other rubbish were removed from the lanes and streets and their holes filled in and levelled; springs and ponds were cleaned; drains were made to dry up marshy places; and adults were taught to write their names. During the Week also the students gave public demonstrations to teach healthy ways of living and ways of storing manure. They organized processions, delivered speeches, sang songs to encourage people to join the adult education centres. In some of the towns the students invited the attention of their local governments to any particularly insanitary places they had noticed and requested that action should be taken to improve them.

We are told that the organizers of these Weeks had expected many adults to resent them or to be sceptical about their purpose and value, but that in the event most people welcomed them and some even joined in the work with the students. 'At one place I found boys and local shopkeepers working shoulder to shoulder to clean up not only the roads and bazaars but shops which, in some cases, had not had such cleaning and scrubbing and fastidious care bestowed on them within living memory.'

This scheme has much to recommend it. The approach is entirely practical. It emphasizes careful preliminary planning with teachers and pupils. It insists that trouble be taken each year to reimpress the students with its underlying objectives and to bring them into the planning as well as the execution of the projects. It presents the school to the community as a corporate body of teachers and students who are also members of the community and willing to work for its general good. It thus helps to allay the natural resentment of the adult at what might otherwise be regarded as presumption on the part of the individual teacher or the individual child. Moreover, after a year or two the Labour Week becomes an annual feature of community life. People come to expect and welcome it rather than resent it. Direct attempts to influence individual adults, which might be resented, are avoided. Any teaching of health and agriculture is done in public for the public, and people feel free to listen or not as they please. Above all, the Labour Week is practical from the teachers' point of view. Although it occurs annually it is limited to a week and during that week they are free from all other duties. They meet the adult community on what is essentially a *school* activity, which is accepted as such by most of the community's adults. They are free from the embarrassment of assuming the teacher's role with their neighbours, and they are supported by the fact that all the teachers in the State are engaged on the same kind of work at the same time. Under these circumstances teachers are much more likely to work with enthusiasm for a week than as unpaid, spare-time extension workers throughout the year.

The idea behind the Labour Week is to take the school to the community, but it may be just as practicable to bring the community to the school. At its simplest this means that the teacher is ready to provide at the school any instruction that he can give and that adults want. Thus he may teach adults to become literate in their own vernacular or in some other desired language, such as English, while the woman teacher may teach the women sewing, knitting, and embroidery. In Samal in the Philippines the women seat themselves at the table on the school verandah. 'The teacher, during lulls in her own work in the classroom, goes out to give instruction to the adult women. The women prefer to remain outside although they have been invited to join the regular class, for they feel they have more freedom to chat outside.'[12] In these and all similar cases, to the degree that the teacher is skilled in adult teaching and is able to meet a need that adults feel, so he or she is helping the people to feel that the school exists also to serve them for their own purposes—that it is *their* community school and not just an outside agency's school.

People are also helped to accept the school as their own—and thus to accept its influence more readily in their lives—if they feel they have some part in organizing it and some say in its affairs. From this point of view even the *Patronato Escolar* (Committee of Adult Patrons of the School) of Guatemala may have some value, although its chief function 'is to provide effective community assistance to the school' by helping in the construction and improvement of school buildings, with the hot lunch programme, and in the provision of paint, whitewash, and similar useful materials. We are told that it was the responsibility of the supervisors of the schools 'to sell the idea of a functional school and the necessity of a parents' and neighbours' organization capable of assuming these responsibilities', that it was successfully 'sold', and that the teachers themselves were surprised by the unsuspected energies thereby generated in the community.[13]

These committees were valuable because they brought together the teachers of the school and the adults of the community to discuss how the community could help the school, thus giving the people some say in school affairs. But the committees become much more valuable when their work is widened to cover also the curriculum, the teachers' aims and methods, the welfare of the children, and the interests of the parents. In very many schools where such committees (usually known as Parent-Teacher Associations or P.T.A.'s) exist, the teachers use them solely to help 'the school', by which they really mean the teachers' idea of what the school should be, and they fear and resent free discussion of what they do and how they do it. Yet the wider the gap between the teacher's idea and the community's idea of what the school should be, the more necessary it is that there should be some means for adults to make their views known and their influence felt. Supervisors and teachers as well as people in the community may need to change their attitude to the school if it is to develop into a community school. This is clearly illustrated by an example taken from the Northern Region of Nigeria.

In 1939 the schools in the Muslim emirates of Northern Nigeria were controlled and supervised by European officers of the central government working through the native administration of each emirate. In theory the schools were administered by the native administrations, but in practice all important policy decisions were made by the agents of the central government. In the eyes of the people the schools were 'government' schools, and the people did not want them. They wanted to keep their children at home to help them on their farms. Thus it was very difficult to enrol even a small class. Attendances were poor and wastage high. Classes in the fourth grade were sometimes left with only three or four pupils. Parents would even send their children away from the village to avoid having them recruited for the school. They feared that it would educate them in the white man's values and ultimately take them out of the community.

In one emirate a serious effort was made to alter this situation. The European supervisor toured the villages to find out what changes were necessary to make the schools more acceptable to the people. He sat down with the elders of each village to discuss this with them patiently, and gradually a more acceptable policy was evolved. It was agreed that no child completing his studies at the village school should be selected for further education without his parents' free consent; that children should enter the school young enough to complete the four-year course at the age of eleven or twelve—the age when their work began to be highly valued on the farm; that there should be much more emphasis on practical farming and handicrafts of use in village life; that the people in each village should have a say in the choosing of the school's religious teacher; that major breaches of discipline involving corporal punishment should be referred to the elders; and that the elders in each village should fix the dates of their school's holidays themselves.

This last point was particularly important since climatic conditions varied greatly in different parts of the emirate, and local variation of holiday dates was essential if children were to be free to help their parents at the busy times on the farms. Administratively, of course, it was highly inconvenient.

By accepting these conditions as reasonable, by implementing them in action, by constituting committees of elders as informal local school committees with the head-teacher as secretary, and by invariably consulting them before making decisions likely to affect school and village relationships, the supervisor helped the people to feel that the school was really theirs. The results were remarkable. Within four years the number of children in school had trebled, the children presenting themselves for admission far exceeded the numbers the schools could take in, attendances improved from 65 per cent. to 80 per cent. and in some cases to 95 per cent., and wastage became negligible. Long-standing opposition to the enrolment of girls also disappeared after the difficulties had been thoroughly discussed with the elders and measures taken to allay their fears, mainly by inviting a trustworthy and locally selected woman to chaperone the girls in school and teach them to cook.

The very great importance of directly involving the adults of the community in the affairs of the school is also well illustrated by what happened in 1936–7 at a school for Indian children in South Dakota in the United States. [14] The teachers felt that they should do something to introduce improvements in the Indian homes from which the children came. The school already had a practice cottage for the girls, and the first step the teachers took was to invite the parents to a meeting to find out what they thought about the home economics teaching, and what they wanted the children to learn that could be of use to them in improving their homes.

Some parents did not think that the practice cottage was of much use, but most of them thought it useful and thought that the boys should have a practice cottage too. They also made suggestions about what the boys and girls should learn, and some parents invited the teachers to come into their homes to see things for themselves. These visits were followed by further meetings, but always the teachers made it clear that it was for the parents and their sons and daughters to decide what needed doing to improve their homes. The teachers were only ready to advise when their advice was sought.

The result of this project, we are told, was the 'overhauling' of each home:

toilets were constructed or improved so that they did not smell and were inaccessible to flies; bedding was washed and aired for the first time in months or ever; partitions were made wherever possible with existing lumber or boxes found under the house, or with moving cupboards or pieces of furniture before the family went to bed at night; the stoves, where there were oil stoves, were cleaned and transferred to places where they were less likely to cause fire; many homes were whitewashed with material that was found a few miles from the village; ventilation was improved etc.

Nor did the effect of the teachers' action stop here:

We, the teachers, surveyed our own homes and decided that we should do a number of things to improve their livability. So did the janitors and bus drivers. We later found that the trader in our community rearranged his own home and the store, and that the priest caused the church to be cleaned and his own house improved.

It is this kind of approach that changes attitudes and prepares the way for mutual learning between the school and the community. The real difficulty here is usually with the supervisor and the teacher. They are accustomed to absolute control over what goes on inside the school and they want to keep it. While they do, the school is their school, not a community school, and its direct and immediate influence on the community is proportionately reduced.

The schools referred to in these examples were rural schools, but the same principles apply to larger urban schools as well. Thus the P.T.A. was a real force in a school of 600 pupils aged six to twelve in Washington, D.C., in the United States.[15] It was highly successful largely because the staff really believed in the necessity of parent co-operation. The Association had sub-committees for special aspects of the school curriculum. These discussed methods of teaching and arranged visits for the children. It sponsored lectures and study groups for the parents. It organized an annual fête to raise funds for books, gramophone records, and other needed equipment. And it organized the use of the school buildings for adult square dancing and drama groups. In effect, the school became a community centre.

In addition at the classroom level the P.T.A. appointed two parents as 'room mothers' to each class to look after the welfare of the children in association with the teacher; it encouraged parents to visit the school during and after school hours; and it developed a scheme of twice-yearly conferences between each individual parent and teacher. The development of the idea of these classroom contacts is itself a good example of the function of the P.T.A., involving as it did parents' meetings which decided to give the suggestion a temporary trial, and a later sampling of parents' opinions on the value of the scheme after they had tried it out.

It is worth noting that in these last examples the neighbourhood committee or P.T.A. is not primarily organized to educate the parents. It exists to facilitate the exchange of information leading to co-operative learning and action to bring school and community together. Ideally the teachers and the parents should meet on equal terms in pursuit of their common objective of the welfare of the children, and they should reach decisions democratically. When this happens the school is directly helping the community to develop by providing a natural centre around which community feeling can grow and find expression. Moreover, if the

P.T.A. is a really democratic and co-operative body it will stimulate local leadership, initiative, and responsibility in dealing with school affairs. We have already noted that it is the development of these qualities in the community that stimulates community development.

In this sense teachers can also help to develop community by establishing more democratic relationships within the school. The good teacher will arrange that groups of children get practice in making decisions for themselves; in working together for the common good, in accepting responsibilitity, and in exercising initiative. In so far as real responsibility is delegated so that children get experience of the difficulties as well as the satisfactions of democratic participation, so one may hope that the school will increasingly feed into the community school-leavers well prepared for membership of adult community groups, and able to play their part in community affairs. 'Schools are communities and school policy must as much as possible be hammered out by the whole school.'[16] In the long run the most effective way the school can contribute to the development of a democratic adult community is by exemplifying democratic relationships within itself.

This is the philosophy that sometimes underlies the modern emphasis on group activity in the classroom, much of which is organized around small group projects of various kinds, and on societies which students learn to run themselves.

Such societies are sometimes specifically related to some aspect of community life and are regarded as a preparation for it. Young Farmers' Clubs, Young Stockbreeders' Clubs, 4–H Clubs, and junior co-operatives are often based on schools, with the teachers acting unobtrusively as leaders. School co-operatives may have many forms and many different aims, such as the purchase of textbooks and stationery; the organization of lunch rooms; the making and selling of handicraft products; the running of the school garden or farm; or the upkeep of the school. 'Examples can be found of school co-operatives which by their example have propagated methods of production giving greater yields, or restored to their locality or region neglected or wasted resources.'[17] But school co-operatives are mainly valued for their aid to schooling. They provide 'centres of interest' around which knowledge acquired in school collects, as well as much other knowledge that cannot easily be fitted into the school curriculum. They develop organizing abilities which ordinary classroom work seldom needs. They also develop social abilities and qualities of self-control and respect for others, always provided that real risks and responsibilities are involved. This is the essential point.

In order to imbue the students with the willingness to make a small sacrifice and to work for an ideal, it was necessary to interest them and to create in them new reasons and motives from which they could derive satisfaction. The greatest of these satisfactions was for them to find themselves treated as adults and no longer as children. When they have reached the stage where they are considered sufficiently adult to collect resources, they should also be sufficiently reasonable and mature to spend such resources and to manage them. The greatest pleasure they derived was through the recognition of this right.[18]

There is one other way in which the school, or rather the school teacher, can influence the community, and this is in his private capacity as a member of it. While it is often unrealistic to expect the teacher to *work* in the community as an unpaid extension agent in addition to his work with children, yet if he lives in the community he will share in community life. He will make friends, he will join community groups, and to the extent that he is better educated than his neighbours, anxious to help them, and unassuming in his manner, so his influence will grow. He can provide a room for meetings; give unobtrusive help with accounts; suggest new activities; and bring in outside help when it is needed. Ideally, he should not seek office or try to retain it. He should aim to help his neighbours help themselves by helping them to learn to organize and run their own activities. Then, when he leaves to take another post, he leaves his neighbours better able to manage their own affairs than when he came. In some tropical territories, such as the West Indies, the best of the rural teachers make their biggest contribution to community development by their membership of co-operatives, agricultural societies, church groups, and many other kinds of voluntary organization.

In all that we have discussed in this chapter we have seen the school and the teacher as important factors in community development provided always that their limitations are recognized. The prime job of the teacher is to make his school a community school, well orientated to the local environment in aim, method, and curriculum; to win the confidence of the people; and to enlist their advice and help in the service of their children. If the teacher succeeds in this he does all that can be fairly expected of him *as a teacher*. If as a member of the adult community he also takes a full but unassuming part in community affairs, serving the community with his knowledge but not trying to direct it, then he will earn the gratitude of the community and will have done well all that he can do. He will have helped to create an 'educated demand' for school education by helping people to see the relation between the teaching of the school, their own betterment, and the development of their community.

In the backward community, however, these developments will take a long time. The untrained, poorly educated teacher who is so common in such areas is the least fitted to carry them out, and even the trained teacher is usually trained only to run an agency-controlled school, not a community school. Teacher-training institutions as well as teachers need to reorientate themselves before we can expect to see a widespread development of the community school, and a bigger contribution by school teachers to the development of the communities their schools should serve. Even when this happens, we must still recognize that the school cannot serve all purposes. Other agencies more directly concerned with adults will still be needed, and we must now discuss in more detail than in the previous chapters the means these other agencies employ.

CHAPTER X

MAKING PEOPLE LITERATE

THE conclusion was reached in the previous chapter that it is unrealistic to expect the school to be able to shoulder the whole burden of community development. Even the best community school will need some help from other agencies and, of course, wherever schools are few and school instruction largely academic, the outside agency is still more badly needed.

One of its most obvious functions is to teach adults how to read and write. There seems to be a direct correlation between illiteracy on the one hand and poverty and high rates of death and disease on the other, and many people feel that the literacy campaign should be made the spearhead of the war on apathy and ignorance which governments and international agencies are now waging in the under-developed areas of the world. Illiterates are shut off from the knowledge contained in books, and while the radio may help, they must mainly depend for new ideas on direct contact with literate people. Unfortunately, the poorer and more backward an area is, the fewer educated people it contains.

If we look back into the history of the mass literacy movement we cannot help noticing that very many of the largest and most successful literacy campaigns were started immediately after some important event in the history of the countries concerned. The Communists in Russia overthrew the Czarist régime in 1917, and within two years Lenin had signed a decree to liquidate illiteracy. Turkey began her literacy campaign almost immediately after Kemal Ataturk had become dictator and president. The vast development of literacy work in India was a direct result of the establishment of the Congress government in power. More recently the big mass literacy campaigns in Indonesia and Ghana, to take only two examples, have been undertaken by the new governments established by successful national independence movements. To a greater or less extent we can also observe the same phenomenon in such countries as Mexico, Thailand, and Burma.

In all these cases the urgent need for making people literate is most clearly seen by the government and by the educated nationalists or revolutionaries who have carried that government into power. 'An illiterate person,' said Lenin, 'is outside the sphere of politics. The first thing he must be taught is the alphabet', and in one way or another every one of the governments mentioned has subscribed to the same idea. They regard a literate people as the only sound foundation on which to build the future of their nation.

This nationalist attitude to literacy has been shared by hundreds of thousands of people in the newly liberated countries. Under its stimulus vast numbers of illiterates have come forward to learn, and many literates have offered to teach without pay. Without the enthusiasm generated by the national liberation movements, of which the mass literacy movement is only one aspect, it may be doubted whether the mass literacy campaigns would be nearly as successful as in fact they are. Even with this stimulus, however, many illiterates do not make the needed effort to learn: some because they do not see the use of learning to read; others because they are too busy with their daily tasks; and others again because they think that reading is too hard for them to learn.

Some of the nationalist governments have been quite prepared to coerce such people. In Russia refusal to attend literacy classes was made punishable by fines, hard labour, loss of food cards, or exclusion from trade unions.[1] In China a law was passed taxing illiterates. In Turkey the government announced that government jobs would only go to people who could read and write. Even today coercion is still sometimes used. Thus after noting some of the difficulties in getting illiterates willingly to learn, the Indonesian Government states in its *Mass Education Handbook*,[2] 'But the facts are that State interests require that every citizen should possess the ability to read and write.' And it therefore tries to force people to become literate by issuing all government notices and orders to the public in writing, by insisting that all forms be filled in by the person directly concerned, and by insisting that every home and place shall have a name board.[3] In one group of Javanese villages, passing a literacy test was even made a requirement for getting permission to marry.[4]

But coercion is not a very satisfactory incentive, and in practice every government tries to find other means of making people want to learn. It aims to demonstrate that reading is *useful*, and that learning to read is *easy*. In one way or another every modern literacy technique has developed from one or other of these two simple ideas.

Although they are easy to state, it is not always easy to say just what should be done to put these ideas into practice. Conditions vary so much, even within the same country, that the methods successfully used in one area may fail in others. In literacy work, as in other forms of community development, success depends on taking each local situation into account.

One of the earliest literacy campaigns was organized among the Muslim Moros of the Lanao Province of the Philippine island of Mindanao by Dr. Laubach of the American Board of Foreign Missions. His first step was to work out simple teaching charts based on the fact that the Maranaw dialect had only twelve consonant sounds and four vowel sounds, and that these were always pronounced phonetically. By selecting three common words which together contained all the consonant sounds and one vowel sound, by breaking these down into syllables, and by then introducing the other three vowels, he found he could teach all the basic elements of reading in three lessons and follow them at once with easy, short sentences. All the learner then needed was practice, which he got by reading *Lanao Progress*, a simple little periodical published by Laubach's agency. Every new literate was urged to read every word of it.

By inventing this 'key word system' Laubach had made it much easier for the Moros to learn, but he also tried to make their learning pleasant. He told his teachers to keep their learners talking, always to ask what they already knew, never to ask questions they could not answer. The teachers must never frown, nor scold, nor look disappointed. They must break down the adult learner's shyness by making him feel that he is astonishingly brilliant.

Simple and pleasant as the learning process had now become, Laubach still had the problem of bringing into the classes the many illiterates who held back, from 'a sense of shame, timidity, fear of the unknown, and superstition', and he tells us how he tried to solve it. He got the teachers to appeal especially to the *datos*, the people's traditional leaders, because they had the power to persuade, and even to compel, the common people to learn. They appealed to the *datos'* pride of race by pointing out that the Moros were behind the other peoples of the world and needed literacy to catch up with them; they appealed to their personal pride by giving certificates and diplomas to the leaders in whose homes everyone had learned to read; and they appealed to their self-interest by suggesting that no *dato* would have any chance of gaining a government post under the new constitution unless the men and women under his influence could write his name on the ballot papers.

They also appealed directly to the common people by printing their lyric and epic poems (of which they were very fond) in *Lanao Progress* and pointing out that only literate people would be able to read them for themselves.[5]

This campaign was a small one compared with later campaigns in other countries, but it was important because Laubach felt that in his 'key word system' he had found something to benefit the great masses of illiterates throughout the world. Thus to his vocation as a missionary of religion Laubach now added a second vocation as a missionary of literacy work based on the new methods. By writing letters, by publishing books, and by extensive tours in Asia, Africa, and Latin America he has done more than anyone else to stir up a world interest in the problem of illiteracy.

Since the Lanao campaign, but more especially since 1945, mass literacy work has been organized in nearly every tropical country. In most cases it has been tackled on much the same lines, and Laubach himself has often been called in to give advice. The first step has been to produce a primer of very easy, graduated lessons; the second, to find teachers, whip up enthusiasm, and organize classes; the third, to publish a simple news-sheet for the people who have just learnt to read.

Unfortunately, experience in many places has shown that this is not enough. Even in some of the most successful areas it was discovered that many of the people who had been taught to read were nevertheless not interested in reading, or at any rate not interested in any of the scanty literature that was provided for them, and that they soon relapsed into illiteracy. Elsewhere, it was sometimes very difficult to get literacy work started at all or, if it did start, to keep people interested long enough to teach them how to read.

These difficulties have forced many literacy workers to rethink their work. Sometimes the trouble was that they had failed to realize that learning to read must be made a pleasant, as well as a technically easy process— a point that Laubach himself had stressed in his Lanao and Indian campaigns, but one which was not always adopted along with his other methods. Thus the Jamaican campaign of 1942 failed because among other reasons:

The wrong type of persons were chosen as instructors. They were chiefly head teachers, mostly men from the urban areas, civil servants, and other highly educated people whose attitude was highly patronizing. They looked down on the illiterates and were far removed in status. Their attitude was unfriendly, and that alienated the people. Then they were termed 'illiterates' which term they resented, as it was so stressed, and this embarrassed them.[6]

It also failed because the Jamaican people did not like Laubach's 'each-one-teach-one' method. They preferred to work in groups.

It was in the Lanao campaign that Laubach got the germ of the idea that later became famous as the 'each-one-teach-one' method. He was short of money to pay his teachers and solved his problem by arranging that as each learner learnt he should teach another. But Laubach and others who uphold this method now support it for quite different reasons. They claim that it avoids all the disadvantages inherent in class teaching.

No time or place needs fixing for class meetings; there is no formal barrier between teacher and learner as there tends to be in a class; and by teaching another person each learner is revising, so to speak, the lesson he has but newly learnt himself. They also claim that the 'each-one-teach-one' method gives the learner the immense psychological satisfaction of being able to help others as others have helped him. Community feeling is strengthened by the practice of mutual aid.

Some literacy workers, however, do not like the system. They point out that the learner is unlikely to teach well what he has only just learnt himself, and that the effectiveness of this kind of teaching depends on the help of an instructor-supervisor being readily available whenever it is needed. It is for this reason that Neijs suggests that the 'each-one-teach-one' method is best suited to areas of dense population where the people are enthusiastic and the work easily supervised. It is less likely, he thinks, to succeed in thinly populated rural areas.[7] This view seems to be borne out by experience in Northern Rhodesia where the Laubach individual method was tried with great success on the Copper Belt, but failed in the much more thinly populated native reserves.

Whatever our views may be about the merits or demerits of group *versus* individual methods of adult literacy work, it is well for us to remember that the learners too may have preferences of their own, and that their wishes should also be considered. Some people much prefer to work in groups. The individual method was not successful in Jamaica. In Tanganyika a literacy organizer encouraged large groups, although he felt they led to bad teaching, because he felt they were good for morale.[8] While in the Gambia:

The question of whether we should use individual or class teaching has been settled for us by the pupils themselves. Fairly early on I had set up an experiment designed to test which of these methods would be most suitable. This was wrecked by the learners themselves. The class and its individual controls overflowed into each other, and nothing I could do prevented it. The method of learning they chose was to come as a group to learn their syllable table and to retire as individuals when they thought they knew enough about it. From then on they worked on their sentences usually alone, but sometimes in pairs or very small groups. It was disconcerting to try to teach a group whose personnel kept constantly changing, but it seemed to be working out all right and we decided that no change was necessary.[9]

It is worth noting that many of the disadvantages of the group method, if that is the method preferred, can be avoided by allowing the learners to form themselves into social groups of their own choosing instead of putting them into formal 'classes'.

The people's convenience must also be considered when choosing a time for the campaign to start. A campaign may fail solely because it is started at a time of the year when the people are busy in their farms and gardens. Nor should a campaign be persisted with too long. This is why literacy work in Ghana is concentrated into only three months of intensive work each year:

This concentration of effort, which is one of the basic principles of mass education, is advocated because of the enthusiasm and publicity which can be focussed on it. Experience here and elsewhere has shown that voluntary groups attempting a continuous effort flag, membership drops, and groups fail through discouragement of leaders and members. The proposals now made provide for an annual revival of enthusiasm and interest.[10]

In every literacy campaign there are many things which can best be decided locally within each small community and preferably by a committee of the community's leaders. If such a committee really is representative and if the people are ripe for literacy work to begin, it can safely be left to find teachers from among the literate adults, fix convenient times and places for teaching to take place, and make arrangements for lamps if the teaching is to take place at night. It is always worth remembering that local arrangements made by a committee of the people who will be affected by them are more likely to suit them than any arrangements made by outsiders, however desirable and efficient such arrangements might seem to be. Local committees should be encouraged to remain in being when the campaign is over, for by organizing further education classes, they can do a great deal to encourage people to go on reading.

In many countries the value of such local committees has never been clearly recognized, and even when they are established they are left without anything worthwhile to do. Even the Unesco Group Training Scheme at Yelwal, Mysore, though recommending that village committees should be set up, nowhere suggests what they should do. Everywhere in its *Literacy Teachers' Guide*[11] it stresses the function of the teacher as the maker of local arrangements, and it assumes, rather surprisingly, that the teacher will not be a member of the community in which he teaches.

While the agency should leave most of the purely local arrangements to be made by the village committee, it must naturally be responsible for supplying the books and other materials needed by the learners. In Ghana this is done very effectively by means of a literacy kit' which contains in one cheap package a primer, an exercise book, a pencil, and a blue and white Mass Education badge. Blue and white are the colours of the Mass Education Movement throughout Ghana and they are used to draw attention to literacy work in every possible way—in the learner's kit, on the vans and lorries, and on the uniforms of the paid workers. When the learner pins on his badge he feels that he is joining a national movement.

The same blue and white colours are also used on the special badges given to every volunteer teacher who has taught a given number of people to read. The badges and the certificates for the new literates are publicly awarded at the celebrations which mark each local Literacy Day. Bands play, visitors flock in from the surrounding villages, congratulatory speeches are made, and the badges and certificates are awarded by some distinguished visitor. No one who has watched the pride on the faces of teachers and new literates as they receive their badges and certificates to the applause of a large crowd of friends and neighbours is likely to underestimate the value of such celebrations in stimulating the will to teach or readiness to learn.* The literacy teacher in Ghana is unpaid. He finds his reward in the enhanced status and respect awarded him by the community.

Most of the volunteer teachers in literacy campaigns have never taught before, and for this reason many agencies arrange short training courses at convenient

* The situation may be entirely different in the mainly literate community where to be illiterate labels a man inferior. Here the illiterate will want to shun the limelight and hide the fact that he cannot read. This is why no literacy classes as such are arranged for illiterates in England. The illiterate who wishes to learn to read and write attends a class for 'General Education'.

local centres. In Ghana such courses last for four or five days. The trainees receive a small daily subsistence allowance and are housed in a schoolroom or other suitable building. The courses are simple and consist of demonstration, practice, and discussion. The teachers are taken through the primer and shown how to teach it. They are also shown how to conduct themselves in class. Bad as well as good lessons are demonstrated, and those who are being trained are asked to criticize them.

In a book on the teaching of reading and writing, W. S. Gray stresses that the teacher should also be trained to prepare adult learners to learn.[12] He should get them to talk over together the advantages that they expect to get from learning to read; correct poor pronunciation; broaden his learners' background of general information; and teach them to express themselves better and think more clearly and to the point. He also suggests that the teacher should register a good deal of information about each learner on index cards or forms and test him to see if he can see and hear properly. Yet however desirable all this may be from a purely professional standpoint one cannot but wonder whether it would work out well in practice. It assumes a professional standard of interest and ability among the volunteer teachers that most of them do not possess; and it would tend to build up the kind of formal relationship between teacher and learners which many agencies deliberately try to avoid. They believe that illiterates learn most easily in an informal social group composed of teacher and learners rather than as students in a 'class'.

By studying the wishes and convenience of the people in every possible way agencies can make learning to read an easy and pleasant process, but this does not completely solve the problem of making people keen to learn or of ensuring that, having learnt, they will want to go on reading.

It is the way this problem is tackled that will decide the ultimate success or failure of a campaign. People differ greatly in their readiness to learn, and the town dweller is usually a keener learner than the peasant. In the town there are signs and posters to be read and letters to be written to the home village. Moreover, the man who can read can often get a better job. Outside the towns the deciding factor is usually the people's stage of social and economic development, and in general the more developed their way of life is, the readier they are to learn to read. Their church may insist on reading as a condition of full membership. Whole communities may want to learn to read in order to establish themselves as 'civilized' communities in the eyes of other people, or for political reasons connected with independence movements. Wherever factors of this kind are present they help to create a climate of 'readiness' in which a literacy campaign has a very good chance of success. The literacy organizer is then helping to satisfy an already existing demand, and the conditions which created this demand will also help to ensure that the new literates will go on reading when they have learned to read.

In backward and isolated areas the situation may be quite different. Many people may never have seen a poster, a signboard, or a news-sheet, and some may not even know what printed symbols are. Such people are quite unready to read, and a serious and long term programme is needed to prepare them for it. Indeed, Gray suggests that a community study should always precede the introduction of literacy classes in order to find out what status reading has in the community; what wider uses could be made of it; what attitudes illiterates have to learning to read; and how the usefulness of reading can most effectively be demonstrated to the people.[13]

This kind of approach to literacy work has too often been neglected, for many agencies have assumed that every illiterate should learn to read regardless of the local situation. They 'sell' literacy to people without inquiring too closely into the uses they can make of it, with the result that they teach people to read but fail to keep them literate.

Of course, everyone agrees that it is wasteful to teach people to read if they quickly become illiterate again, and that the real aim must be to make people *functionally* literate so that they will regularly make use of reading and writing in their daily lives. But most agencies have tried to ensure this by stressing the importance of follow-up literature rather than by stressing that people must be prepared for learning to read. Thus in nearly every country there is now much emphasis on the production and distribution of popular news-sheets and cheap and simple books and booklets intended for the new literates, and as more and more of these are produced it is assumed that new literates will read them and not relapse.

To some extent this is true, but it does not always work out well in practice. While some new literates are so keen on reading that they will struggle through almost anything produced for them, many others will only read if the literature is cheap, attractively produced, closely related to their interests, and *locally* available. Unfortunately, much of the literature produced fails to satisfy all these conditions, and much therefore remains in offices and stores unread. The real

V. TEACHING ADULTS TO READ

Above. A village learns to read. *Below.* Even the old take part

VI. A WOMAN MASS EDUCATION OFFICER

Above. Addressing the people.   *Below*. Taking part in a village dance

answer to this problem lies, as Gray suggests, in study-ing each local community, encouraging people to develop specific interests in reading and uses for it, and producing follow-up literature which satisfies these interests. It is wasteful to teach people to read until they know what they want reading for.

It is necessary to labour this point because it is much easier to get people to learn to read than to keep them reading. Even in very backward communities people have been stimulated to learn to read by means of clever propaganda and appeals to their emotions with-out their having any idea of what use they can make of reading when they can read. Appeals to national pride can be used in this way with great effect in newly liberated countries.

The temptation to base a literacy campaign on an emotional appeal of this kind should be carefully avoided. It is valuable as a secondary incentive only. The main appeal should always be based on the actual uses people will be able to make of reading in their daily lives.

In isolated and backward areas these are often negli-gible, especially if there is hardly any printed literature already published in the local language, and it is usually better to postpone active literacy work in such places until a good supply of suitable literature for new liter-ates to read can be assured. Meanwhile, it is useful to concentrate on other kinds of development such as the building of roads and markets and the improvement of agriculture. People will be more ready to read, and get more benefit from reading, when these other forms of development have created more local uses for it.

Elsewhere, the organizer's first task is to stimulate a greater interest in reading. Gray suggests[14] that he should arrange village meetings and group meetings, e.g. with co-operative and church groups likely to be specially interested in reading, to discuss the uses that people can make of reading. At such meetings 'the values of literacy are discussed, the ability of recent literates to read is demonstrated, and the fact is emphasized that one can learn to read in a relatively short time'. At such meetings, too, an illiterate can be given his first lesson in reading to show him and his friends how very easy it is. Gray also recommends that bulletin boards be set up in the villages with leaflets and papers attached to them, and literate adults encouraged to read them to illiterates. Preparatory work of this kind, he suggests, should be continued until enough interest has been aroused for a village literacy committee to be formed to make detailed local arrangements for a campaign. The working of this committee provides the first real test of the community's readiness for reading. If it fails to find learners and teachers or to make arrangements for the classes to be held, it probably means that the agency has not yet succeeded in its first essential task of ensuring that the people really want to read.

Getting people to discuss the uses they can make of reading is useful in another way, for it helps the organizers to discover what kind of follow-up reading is likely to interest the people most, and thus avoid the risk of producing the wrong kind of literature. It also helps them to avoid the kind of error made recently in Malaya where a campaign was launched to teach people to read their own language in the Roman script. In some areas, e.g. Trengannu, the people had no use for it. They preferred their own Jawi script because their newspapers and other literature were already published in it, and they valued the Roman script only for learning to read in English. The campaign was therefore out of touch with the people's needs, and no amount of propaganda could overcome this handicap.

Like every other pioneer in a new field of work the literacy organizer has had to learn from experience, and in the course of learning make mistakes. But three main principles now seem well established: (i) that people must be helped to realize how reading can help them in their daily lives; (ii) that people must be provided with the kind of reading that they really want; and (iii) that the first step in really backward areas must be to create uses for reading by going ahead with a general development programme before the literacy worker comes in. Agencies working along these lines no longer see literacy as an end in itself. They see it as one of several complementary approaches to a broad policy of community development.

How the agency carries out the first and third functions has already been briefly discussed; the second presents a rather more complex problem. It is sometimes hard to know what people would really like to read, difficult to produce cheap and attractive literature for each small language area, and still more difficult to get it to the people where they live.

One of the most useful reading materials for the new literate is a cheap, clearly printed, and regularly published news-sheet—always provided that the people are really interested in reading it.

It is often hard for the editor of such a news-sheet to bridge the cultural gap between himself and his potential reading public of new literates, especially if he lives in a town and most of his readers are country folk. His task is harder still if he has to produce the news-sheet for a very large area, for newly literate people are usually interested mainly in the one small district where they live. They like to read about people and places they know and to feel that the news-sheet is really meant for them.

One answer to this difficulty may be to produce special editions of the same news-sheet, each edition carrying its own page or two of purely local news. Another is to make *Letters from our Readers* a very prominent feature of each issue. This is the policy, in fact, which has been largely responsible for the great success of the Northern Nigerian paper *Jakadiya*. A special edition is produced for several different areas, and letters from readers figure prominently in each issue.*

Letters from readers and local news also contributed greatly to the success of a small news-sheet produced for the pastoral Nandi people of Kenya.

The most difficult, though in some ways the most rewarding, contributions come on vintage scraps with unaccustomed hand and unguided nib and mixed dialect, the opinions and the questions of the just-literate being saved from the descent into inarticulacy. . . . Even the simplest newspaper has a very real contribution to make to community development. By disseminating views as well as news, by stimulating interest in local culture and the common welfare it can widen the reader's horizon in every way.[15]

And it does so all the more effectively, we may believe, by encouraging, editing, and printing the faltering first efforts of the new literates themselves.

Next in importance is the production and distribution of short, cheap, and clearly printed books, preferably illustrated, certainly with an attractive cover, and

---

* It is interesting to note that the existence of some old cave drawings near Birnin Kudu in Kano province first came to light as the result of a letter written to the paper by a new literate.

with a content which interests new literates and stimulates them to read.

Field workers can often produce local news-sheets as a sideline to their other activities, but successful large-scale campaigns create a potential demand for literature which can only be met by employing whole-time editors and other production staff, and in some parts of the tropics this has meant the setting up of literature bureaux. A single bureau may produce news-sheets, periodicals, pamphlets, and books in many dialects and languages.

Running a bureau is costly and difficult, and it calls for much greater skill and resources than the relatively straightforward literacy campaign. The bureau has to try to create a reading public out of new literates, and this is a far harder task than to produce books for a public whose reading tastes are known. The bureau has to face the problem of assessing what kind of reading the new literates want. Here even experienced field workers can make mistakes. Thus the organizers of literacy work in North Pare co-operated with the East African Literature Bureau in producing a small pamphlet on pottery which they thought would sell well among the women who made the local pots. It did not sell, and Mason notes that they were still far from discovering the best kind of follow-up literature for women.[16] The only other available literature consisted of a series of small pamphlets on Trees, Hides and Skins, and Food and Cattle, but these were too sophisticated for the people to find much interest in reading them.

The difficulty of producing literature which really will be read is all the greater when, as until recently in Ghana, the bureau which produces the reading materials has no close and continuous contact with literacy workers in the field.

Bureaux also commonly have much difficulty in getting literature sold in the villages. There are few shops in most underdeveloped areas, and still fewer shop-keepers who are willing to stock books and pamphlets unless they know they will have a quick and ready sale for them.

There have been many attempts to solve this problem. In several parts of Africa lorries have been fitted up as mobile bookshops to carry books to the people in rural areas, and especially to places, such as markets, where people meet in large numbers on particular days. Many books have been sold by this means in Uganda[17] and Nigeria,[18] but in some countries it has been found too costly for general use. Attempts have also been made to sell books through school teachers and by means of colporteurs working on a commission basis, but none has proved really satisfactory.

It is doubtful whether this problem will ever be satisfactorily solved while it is primarily regarded only as a problem of book distribution. The real problem is to make people *want* the books enough. Soap, matches, pocket mirrors, knives, and many other cheap articles already reach even the remotest villages of the backward areas, however difficult it may be to get them there, just because people really want them and will buy them from the traders who bring them. What is true of soap and mirrors can also be true of books, always provided that people find them useful and therefore want them.

If people have real purposes in learning to read they will have real needs for reading which can be supplied by books, and the existing problems of distribution only serve to underline the importance of soundly preparing people to read before the literacy campaign is launched. Literacy work involves the agency in far more work than merely organizing the campaign. Before the campaign starts, as we have seen, the agency must be sure that the people are ready for it. When it is over, the learners must be encouraged to discuss how their reading needs can best be met, and encouraged, too, to stay together in classes or reading circles to further their education. Sometimes church, co-operative, and other groups can be invited to form study and reading groups of their own. It can then be left to the group representatives and to the village literacy committee to work out ways and means of getting needed news-sheets and books into the groups thus formed. In literacy work, as in many other fields, it is easy to overlook the value of the group. It is natural for people to organize themselves to carry out their purposes, and if people are interested enough in reading they will form groups which can help to organize the demand for books and thus solve the distribution problem. The group or reading circle with its regular meetings is also useful in helping the new literate to acquire the *habit* of reading, and it is worth noting that groups can be provided with book-boxes and study-boxes. By this means one other hindrance to the development of functional literacy in individuals—the cost of buying books for individual use —is largely overcome. Each group member has cheap access to a number of books, and the group can provide the stimulus to use them and discuss them.

Literacy work is usually most successful when it is geared in with a broader programme of community development, for such development often creates new uses for reading and writing, especially if it stimulates small purpose groups such as co-operatives and groups of farmers. The Jamaican Agricultural Society provides a good example of this, for it is an active, flourishing society with local branches all over the island, even in some of the poorest parishes. It aims to help the people to help themselves, and it publishes a journal to teach them better ways of farming. But not all of them can read. Thus in 1953 a group of young men in the district of Marlborough, unable to read the journal because they were illiterate, asked their local schoolmaster to teach them. The idea caught on so well that several hundred people learned to read, and the idea spread to other districts. The value of such indirect approaches to literacy through extension work of other kinds is sometimes overlooked. Though its results may be less spectacular, they are often more lasting than those obtained by the straight mass literacy campaign.

While many forms of development can thus help to stimulate a demand for literacy the reverse is also true, for literacy work can stimulate other kinds of development. The literacy class at Kinondoni built an evening school, founded a football club, and organized inter-village sports. At Ogwofia in Eastern Nigeria it was the stimulus of finding that they were able to learn to read that started the people off on a whole series of other community projects.[19] And it was literacy work in North Pare which, without ever becoming a mass movement, 'produced a climate favourable for the anti-erosion and tree-felling campaign'.[20]

If we take note of such developments we no longer see literacy as an isolated activity but as an integral part of community development. Literacy work interacts with many other community activities, stimulating them or being stimulated by them, and the criteria for successful literacy work are the same as for all other forms of community development. The better the people understand why they want to become literate and the more they can be encouraged to take over responsibility for making their own local arrangements, the more likely they are to value their ability to read and write once they have acquired it: and the more likely they are to become *functionally* literate.

CHAPTER XI

INTRODUCING NEW IDEAS

A T one time many people saw the literacy campaign as the 'spearhead' of progress in underdeveloped areas, but experience has led them to take a more sober view. This is especially true of backward areas where there is no widespread *lingua franca*, where it is difficult and costly to produce and distribute books, where most literates are slow and stumbling readers, and where many people still cannot read at all. Yet it is in just these places that governments most want to influence people to safeguard their lands against erosion, adopt new farming methods, and learn how to avoid preventable disease. Fortunately, the printed word is only one way of reaching people with new ideas, and not necessarily the best, even for people who can read. It is difficult to explain new ideas clearly and briefly if only words are used, and harder still when the words are in books which, unlike teachers, cannot answer questions or clear up misunderstandings.

This is one reason why books become more useful if people study them in groups. If several people read the same book they can help each other to understand it by discussing it and answering each other's questions about it. Moreover, group study is usually far more effective than individual reading in stimulating people to act. Once the members of a group have decided in favour of a new idea, each member feels strengthened by the support of the others in carrying it out.

Pictures can often convey meaning better than words, especially if the pictures are drawn to represent ideas and relations between ideas as clearly and simply as possible. It is with this in mind that the Government of the Western Region of Nigeria has published a number of small books and posters in collaboration with the Isotype Institute of Great Britain. Each is issued in several of the main languages of the region, and on each page is a large picture accompanied by one or two lines of text. Most of the meaning is contained in the pictures which are carefully related to one another and to the local culture. The words are few and present no difficulty to the new literate. Even the illiterate, once he has had the pictures explained to him, can go on studying and learning from the pictures without troubling about the text.*

Isotypes make books more useful as carriers of ideas

* Note, however, that the value of pictures, charts, and diagrams to help the reader visualize meaning can easily be over-estimated, especially among people who have but newly learnt to read. Like writing, pictures, charts and diagrams convey meaning by means of symbols, and people have first to learn to understand the symbols, just as they originally have to learn to read. (See M. D. Vernon, 'Presenting Information in Diagrams', *Audio-Visual Communication Review*, Vol. 1, 3, 1953.)

by conveying meaning in pictures which near-illiterates can understand. Broadcasting avoids the barrier of illiteracy altogether. Radio programmes can be heard by people who cannot read. Indeed, they are sometimes used as a means of teaching people how to read.[1] They are especially useful for reaching small and scattered populations whom it would be expensive to try to educate by any other means. It is partly for this reason that such store is set by educational broadcasting in Northern Rhodesia and in Brazil, where there are immense tracts of country with a population of about one per square mile.

In spite of its great advantages broadcasting cannot provide any easy, simple solution to problems of influencing adults in the tropics, even where people can listen to the programmes. The programmes will only be effective if people can be attracted to listen to them, can understand them, and can see how they can apply the lessons of the programmes to their daily lives. It is by no means easy for the programme providers to ensure that these conditions are always met.

No one can be made to listen to an educational broadcast any more than he can be made to buy and read a book. People can switch off their set or change over to another and possibly more entertaining programme. Equally, they can hear the programme without listening to it. Many people in the tropics, like many people in Western countries, leave their sets on to provide a background of sound for whatever they may be doing about the house. To get people really to *listen* to a programme in the home is one of the major difficulties of the educational broadcaster.

One way of overcoming this difficulty is to encourage people of like interests, such as farmers or housewives, to form their own groups to listen to programmes specially prepared to interest them, and to stay on after each programme to discuss it. In some countries such groups are helped with printed materials carefully designed to explain and support the programmes. Thus in Brazil housewives are supplied with books and pamphlets on food, and cooking, and food canning: while farmers are supplied with printed materials on animal-raising, planting seasons, and the harvesting of crops.[2] In such cases the wireless programmes are used to stimulate and help people to undertake a pre-arranged course of group study.

People must not only listen to educational programmes, they must be helped to understand them and appreciate them if they are to be influenced by them. Thus the educational broadcaster, like every other adult educator, must know a great deal about the way the people of his audience live and how to put his teaching into a form that they can understand. Grenfell Williams stresses how difficult it is to illustrate new ideas and alien concepts in ways that people can really understand. He suggests that it is generally better to avoid the straight lecture or talk. It is essential to achieve simplicity while avoiding any suggestion of condescension. 'Condescension, patronage of any kind, show up starkly in the disembodied voice coming out of the loud-speaker' and will be strongly resented.[3] It is for this reason that he favours the technique of the dramatized story,[4] and of the question and answer programme in which the listener can identify himself or herself with one of the persons who questions the 'expert'.[5]

It is fortunate that two of the most important fields for adult education in the tropics—home economics and health education—are both well suited to the kind of programme that presents a good radio personality to play the part of the radio cook, the radio nurse, or the radio doctor; and that broadcasting gets directly into the home to the women for whom the programmes are intended. It is claimed in Brazil that women listen to the radio for more hours than any other group.

Broadcasting, like the printed word, is mainly useful for introducing people to new ideas and preparing them for change. This is also true of films, and most governments now use some kind of mobile cinema for showing films to people in the villages. Films have many advantages over print and broadcasting as a means of propaganda. Film shows are popular in rural areas so that there is usually no difficulty in collecting a crowd and focussing attention on the screen; and the film is a good medium for telling a story which appeals to the emotions of the audience. Indeed when it suggests an easy and immediate answer to a strongly felt want it may even arouse an immediate response. The Nigerian film *Smallpox* is a film of this kind, and wherever it is shown in areas affected by the disease it is always necessary to have vaccinators ready to deal with people from the audience who come forward for treatment.

Unfortunately films are costly to make though relatively cheap to show, so that a film is usually shown over a very wide area, sometimes even in countries many thousands of miles away from the country for which it was primarily intended. Thus most of the films that people see show backgrounds of habit, dress, and locale quite different from their own, and audiences are often more interested in the differences between the actors in the film and themselves than in the lesson the film is intended to teach. At one time this was felt to be a major drawback in the use of films, but Norman Spurr has noted that this does not invariably happen, *provided the film deals with a problem of vital interest to the people and offers an acceptable solution to it.*[6] He suggests that a film which satisfies these two conditions can be used effectively in other cultures, and he gives the films *Smallpox* and *Trees are Cash* as examples of this kind of film. On the other hand, he notes that a film on cattle-dipping which was successful among the people for whom it was made failed among another pastoral people in the same territory. This tribe realized that cattle-dipping would also involve cattle-counting and they were afraid of the government taxing their cattle. To them the message of the film was therefore unacceptable.

Some of the inevitable disadvantages involved in using foreign films can be avoided by turning down the foreign sound-track and substituting a really good local commentary.[7] This is a view strongly held by workers in Ghana.

'The vernacular commentary', they say, 'should be thoroughly worked out and strictly adhered to, which will (a) make sure that the action of the film is thoroughly understood; (b) transpose the whole story into the African scene by giving local names to rivers and forests and people; (c) lay special emphasis on those points which are particularly difficult for the African audience to believe.'[8]

This quotation of Shirer and Pickering refers especially to research experiments carried out to test the usefulness of showing the Walt Disney cartoon health films in Ghana, and the conclusions based on these experiments closely coincide with the results of similar experiments conducted by Norman Spurr with the same films in Uganda.[9] Both stress the importance of cutting out the original sound-track and replacing it with a good vernacular commentary. Both conclude that the cartoon film with a good local commentary is a remarkably effective teaching aid, and that it has great advantages over the ordinary kind of film. People, they find, can more easily identify themselves with the story of the cartoon film because neither the background nor the characters of the film have nationality, though they and their story are recognizably human and credible. [10]

Thus there is at least some evidence that films designed for one area of the tropics can be used in other quite different areas. But it is still true that there are as yet relatively very few really suitable films available. There are several reasons for this. One is that film technicians, most of whom have been trained in the West, need special additional training before they can make good films for rural people in the tropics. The test of a good film is its effectiveness with the audiences for which it was designed rather than the winning of a film award for excellence by Western standards. Norman Spurr illustrates this point by describing the attitude of students at the British Colonial Office's Film Training School to a film that had been made in the tropics. They criticized the continuity, acting, direction, and photography of the film. Their major interest centred on the techniques, but 'we were able to point out that the film had been completely successful and largely responsible for the stopping of petty thieving of crops on the island concerned'. [11]

A second reason is that some tropical film production units spend a disproportionate amount of time and effort in producing films *describing* community development work and primarily designed for audiences outside the territory concerned. Although these films are often shown to village audiences, they do not deal with village development with the village audience in mind, and they are largely ineffective for that reason.

Even those films which are specially made for village audiences are sometimes unsuitable. Some exaggerate bad conditions in the villages in order to stress the need for change. The audience's reaction is then to think that they are better than the people shown in the film and that its message does not really apply to them. Other films appeal too much to fear, painting the dangers of neglect too harshly, and leading people to close their minds to facts made too unpleasant. Others, again, use ridicule. Thus the Northern Rhodesian film *The Two Farmers* pours scorn on the unprogressive farmer, who is shown as lazy and incompetent, while exaggerating the benefits reaped by the farmer who takes the agricultural demonstrator's advice. This film might have been more effective among the unprogressive farmers for whom it was presumably intended if it had shown a sympathetic demonstrator patiently encouraging and helping such a farmer slowly to make good in spite of his initial, unco-operative attitude.

One need, then, is to get more good films especially designed for rural audiences in the tropics. This is being met by training film technicians to produce them. But field workers also need to appreciate the good and bad points of the films they use. Ideally the film should be the product of a two-way traffic of ideas between the field worker who uses films and the technician who makes them.

Workers also need to know which of the many existing films they ought to show, for it is a mistake to show people bad films, 'bad' that is in the sense that the

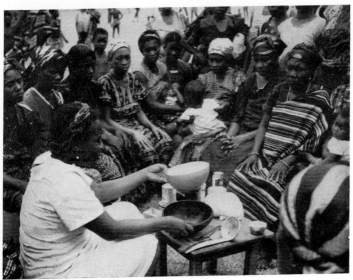

VII. HOMECRAFT TEACHING

Above. In East Africa.   *Below.* In West Africa

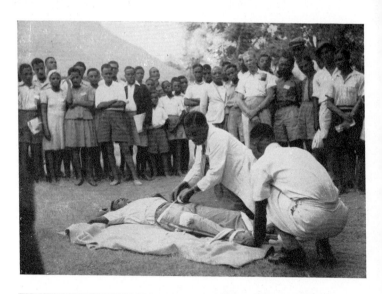

VIII. TRAINING VOLUNTARY WORKERS

Above. Training people near their homes (*see page* 215)
Below. A district training centre (*see page* 211)

audiences are not interested in them or do not understand them. One way of avoiding this is to try films out on pre-viewing committees of local people who are reasonably representative of the expected audiences.

This is a technique which was successfully used by Jean and Jess Ogden when selecting films on nutrition for Greene County, Virginia, U.S.A. in 1942.[12] It has also been used successfully in Trinidad, where a committee of local people select the films for showing and draft a short account of each, together with suggestions for putting into practice 'the good points shown in the film and practicable in Trinidad'. Local Cinema Reception Committees arrange for groups of people to study these outlines before the films are shown, and local experts are asked to attend the showing of the films as guest speakers. These arrangements were from the start a 'tremendous success'. The use of the guest speaker was, we are told, particularly successful. It was his job to clarify the message of the film and to bring its implications home to the people in relation to themselves.[13] Shirer and Pickering also stress that films should be shown to small key audiences in each village or area before they are shown to the general public.[14]

The use of such simple techniques as these—the selection of films by a pre-viewing committee, the preparation of a good *local* commentary or sound-track, the talk by the guest speaker, and the ensuing discussion—can enormously enhance the educational value of the showing of films, but, like the printed word and the radio, the film's main function is to stimulate interest and to help to make people ready for change. It can stimulate action only when the change proposed is simple and easy, like vaccination against smallpox. Where the suggested change is of a more complex kind, or involves the people in making some major effort or sacrifice, a much more personal approach is needed, and success depends on the personality of the field worker, the relationship he has established with the people, and his ability to explain and demonstrate, to answer questions, to resolve local doubts and difficulties, and to move people from interest to action. Press, film, and radio can help, but in the end we must recognize them as 'aids' to the worker rather than as prime movers of the people to action.

This point is well brought out in an account of a recent, large-scale campaign in Ghana. Cocoa is Ghana's main export, but for some years the crop has been seriously threatened by disease. Previous attempts to get farmers to take the Agricultural Department's advice had largely failed.

The new campaign was sponsored jointly by the Department of Social Welfare and Community Development, whose staff were experts in mass education techniques, and by the Department of Agriculture, which supplied the technical staff. Senior officers of both Departments co-operated closely in planning the campaign and in training field workers for it.

Great trouble was taken to provide the field workers with effective aids. Paper materials included eight designs of poster, discussion sheets, and a pictorial broadsheet addressed to cocoa farmers in five vernacular languages and in English. News items and programmes about the campaign were featured on the radio. Three thousand copies were made of a special dance tune 'Cocoa Highlife' recorded for the gramophone by a well-known Ghana dance band, and the records were distributed free to cinemas, bars, and other institutions. Played over a loudspeaker, they were found very useful for collecting crowds during the campaign.

The field workers were also supplied with four 16mm. films, each dealing with one of the four major objectives of the campaign. The films were shown from seven mobile cinema vans and at four Rural Training Centres. We are told that these films helped to stimulate interest among the people and thus to make the work of the Mobile Demonstration Teams much easier.

The Mobile Demonstration Teams stayed for three or four days in each village. They demonstrated the recommended sprayers and showed film-strips on each of the four objectives of the campaign. These film-strips were used with small groups of village farmers to explain to them in some detail the nature of the diseases which attacked their cocoa. The teams also gave short, simple plays against a plain backcloth and these were found very useful, especially where the people were initially slightly hostile. Hand puppets were successfully used in Ashanti.

Much trouble was taken to interest chiefs, other local notabilities, and cocoa-buyers, and to get them to take an active part in the campaign.

In a campaign where the workers are using aids of many kinds they cannot with certainty single out any one as more effective than the rest. But one gets the impression from the account of the campaign that more people were convinced by seeing the spray demonstrations than in any other way. We are told, for instance, of a doubting farmer who arrived at a meeting with four live capsids in a match-box, and who produced them at the appropriate moment in the hope of confounding the government officers. When within a few minutes of being sprayed they were dead, 'The villagers yelled with delight at this operation and poured £2 notes on us for the purchase of Mysto sprayers'. [15] The live demonstration is usually the simplest, and also the cheapest and most effective visual aid whenever it can be appropriately used.

The campaign met with such quick success that within two months between 3,000 and 4,000 farmers had applied to purchase sprayers (a demand that unfortunately could not at once be met). One reason for this success was undoubtedly the care taken in planning and producing a wide variety of different aids and ways of approaching the people. But a still more important factor was the excellence of the relations which officers of the Social Welfare and Community Development Department had established with the people as the result of their earlier work. 'Through their continued association with the villagers in their literacy work, our staff have built up a feeling of mutual trust between themselves and the people, which only they possess. This is the key factor of success in any campaign, however difficult. . . .' [16] It is also worth noting that the account of this campaign concludes 'that the most important work lies ahead. The Cocoa farmer must not only be convinced of the importance of employing modern methods *but he must be persuaded to use them as a matter of routine.*' [17]

This highlights the basic problem of all extension work and also the limitations of the campaign method of the kind outlined above. The campaign is often the best, and sometimes the only way of introducing innovations quickly, but though it is intensive it is also short. If it is to have a permanent effect it must be followed up by less spectacular but more continuous work. Moreover, the campaign method can only be used to emphasize the few key changes most urgently required, whereas most rural development programmes involve small changes of many different kinds.

One way of coping with this problem is the Movable School. This consists of any wagon, car, or lorry that can carry simple equipment for demonstrations and one or two people to demonstrate it. This technique was first sponsored from the Tuskegee Institute by Dr. Booker T. Washington in 1906 as a means of reaching, at their homes, impoverished negro farmers who could not easily be reached by any other means, and it has been continued and developed ever since. The whole emphasis of the Movable School is to help people to help themselves in improving homes and farms, and the most important local detail in preparing for such a school is the selection of a suitable place.

'The house selected', we are told, 'should represent the average in a given community. Another important feature in selecting a place for the Movable School is that the place chosen should offer an advantage of teaching the greatest number of lessons in and around the home. It is also very important that the occupants of the home selected are on friendly terms with the rest of the community. Otherwise poor attendance is likely to result.'[18]

In return for agreeing to the use of his home and farm as a classroom, and supplying the materials needed to make improvements, the farmer benefits from the work done during the course of the school. The whole scheme is devised to take education to the rural people in the form they can most easily accept and under conditions that ensure that they learn effectively by doing. It is said that the Movable School stimulates the social life of people in backward communities as well as teaching them to make improvements on their farms and in their homes.

H. N. Silvera has described an experiment to adapt this technique to conditions in Jamaica.[19] In 1947 Jamaica Welfare had already considerably developed its extension work with village groups, but was seeking ways of reaching the many people, usually those most in need of help, who were not members of the organized groups with which it worked. A Welfare Car was therefore equipped with cooking utensils, a sprayer for use with plants and another for spraying latrines, a pair of pure-bred Leghorn chickens with samples of their eggs for comparison with eggs from common fowls, a first-aid kit, a handyman's kit for the home, exhibits of local handicrafts and preserved foods, a film-strip projector, and posters and free literature for distribution. The idea was to teach by demonstration, using the articles carried in the car, and animals, etc., borrowed on the spot. Teaching was done in the open air, and the people were collected by community singing.

Both Silvera and Marier stress the value of this technique. Experience in Jamaica has shown that workers coming back tired and dirty from their farms, with ragged clothes and carrying their tools, will not attend indoor functions, although they will loaf around outside. These people were reached by the Movable School because it did not embarrass them, and because it presented its programme in a way that interested them. It was estimated that 60 per cent. of the people who attended these schools had not been seen in either clubs, community centres, churches, or any other kind of organized group. To this extent the Movable School reached a new audience.

Local exhibitions and fairs are another means of

interesting people in improving the way they run their homes and farms, but whether they educate people or not depends very much on the way they are organized. An exhibition only provides *opportunities* for educating people together with incentives to encourage them to learn, and the exhibition is of educational value only to the extent that these opportunities are used. It is not enough merely to collect exhibits, judge them, and award the prizes. Other factors such as the size and situation of the exhibition can affect its educational value. The small, local exhibition held in a rural setting usually provides more opportunities for educating rural folk than the big and grandiose exhibition in or near the town.

Exhibitions bring large numbers of people together in a setting where they can be educated, and they can then be educated in two ways. On the one hand they can have demonstrated to them new ideas, new tools, new crops, new methods of farming, new gadgets for the home, and new dishes for the housewife to prepare: on the other they can be interested in the qualities the judges look for in the animals, crops, and craftwork entered for the competitions.

One attempt to work along these lines was made in the Indian village of Nitaya. A voluntary agency already working in the village organized a three-day fair on a harvested pea field lent for the purpose by one of the villagers, and from the start the villagers co-operated with the agency workers in preparing for it.[20]

The lay-out of the fair was simple: a long building of poles and bamboo mats along two sides of a square, the school building on the third side, and the fourth side open where animals could be exhibited. The centre of the square was used for demonstrations and part of it was roofed over for meetings.

About half the total space was allocated to the school and to government organizations for their exhibits and demonstrations, and the other half to the exhibits of the villagers. The nearest government farm showed models of improved tools, and demonstrated a sugar production unit and tractor cultivation. The soil conservation department showed how to care for chickens, which only a few villagers had previously kept. The school demonstrated weaving and exhibited some of the woven articles the pupils had made. The agency itself showed the large variety of vegetables it grew at its own local centre; a model confinement room, village style; and a model latrine. It also demonstrated the proper way to make a compost pit, a bore-hole latrine, a soak-pit, and a wash place where the water ran into a garden. Unfortunately, we are not told in detail how these were demonstrated to ensure that the people really understood them.

The exhibits of the villagers occupied the remaining space. These were divided into four groups: animals; handicrafts; produce and grains; and women's work. Fifty-eight people entered animals; eighty or ninety exhibited produce and grains; forty women exhibited in the women's section; and twenty people exhibited handiwork. In every section most exhibitors entered more than one exhibit.

The judging was done by local experts from the Centre or from government departments, and a good deal of trouble was taken to help people understand the basis on which the judging was done. A score-card was prepared for each group of judges, and the details of these score-cards were printed and widely circulated before the fair in the hope that the exhibitors would use them when deciding on their entries. The organizers had also aimed to have the judging done in front of the crowd, to display before each first prize exhibit a list of the reasons for giving it the first prize, and to hold a meeting where each first prize winner would be interviewed about his exhibit. They failed to do so, we are told, because faulty organization of the judging left too little time, but the organizers still felt that these ideas were worth persisting with in future exhibitions.

It was for this fair that the village people revived their traditional Bullock Cart Race, which attracted a crowd of 5,000 to 6,000 people. Nearly all these people visited the fair before or after the race. In addition, on each of the first two evenings, a play was produced before audiences of over a thousand people.

One can well believe that this small local fair had a very considerable educational influence on the people of Nitaya and its surrounding villages, and in many aspects of village life; and that it would have had much more had the organizers had the skill to carry out fully their original intention. It was more representative of the small rural community than large district or provincial fairs could hope to be, it enlisted the people's active participation, and it attracted people *to the village*, rather than out of it to the town. This small fair was also cheap. We are told that it cost only 700 rupees for everything, including the rent of building materials, prizes, printing, food for the staff, and other incidentals.

In all, twenty-seven small prizes were awarded, but in addition *every* exhibitor received a certificate and a ribbon. 'The next day, we saw several people in fields and on the roads with our ribbons pinned to them. We felt satisfied that these ribbons and certificates were the right idea and that the exhibitors were pleased to receive them.' Thus at Nitaya two ideas were represented—the competitive prize to reward excellence in individual exhibits, and the certificate to award status to every exhibitor. Both were intended as incentives, and each has a different appeal. Prize awards to individuals are almost universally acceptable in Western competitive society, but are less acceptable in some rural communities in the tropics, especially in those which are still mainly dominated by tradition. The people in such communities may value a certificate as a symbol shared with others, but dislike being singled out for an individual competitive award.[11] In such cases the award of certificates to most or all exhibitors will provide a more powerful incentive than the award of prizes.

The Movable School and the local exhibition enable workers easily to meet and influence large numbers of people at small expense, but neither they nor the more expensive set campaign provide the permanent stimulation that is so often needed. In the end, the main burden of introducing change has usually to be shouldered by the field worker in his day-to-day contacts with the people. As such workers are very few in relation to the large numbers of people they have to try to influence, they need all the help and support their agency can provide.

The prime need of the extension worker is for a 'saleable' programme, well related both to people's needs and their resources. This he does not always get. In one part of Latin America health workers not unnaturally failed when they had to try to get people to install seat privies where the local custom was to squat, and in another they failed to get householders to adopt a type of privy which cost ten dollars to install. Ten dollars may have seemed a reasonable enough price to the agency which framed the programme, but it was quite impracticable among the rural people for whom it was intended. 'Since the people's least expensive *houses* were worth only from 18 to 35 dollars, the chances of success were naturally very small.'[22]

The need to understand people's way of life and the reasons they have for doing what they do is still more strikingly illustrated by an example from India, where in a certain district difficulty was encountered in getting the people to make latrines or improve their wells. The source of the difficulty was finally traced to the young women in purdah who believed that if latrines were made in their homes they would lose their one and only regular opportunity of going out of their houses, meeting their friends, and getting a change of air. In this district women did not visit each other's houses. They went out only to draw water or 'sit in the jungle', and they prized these outings far more highly than purer water or more hygienic sanitation. Dr. Gladys Rutherford who provides this illustration visualizes a solution in a 'Women's Sunrise Club' where hygienic toilet and washing facilities could be provided, together with the opportunities for social intercourse which the women want.[23]

What this and similar examples teach us is that the factors affecting success or failure in extension work may lie quite outside the sphere of the extension agency's main interest, and it is for just this reason that they are so often overlooked. For the people, most innovations have demerits as well as merits, and people will only willingly accept a change when they are convinced that the good outweighs the bad. It is not enough for them that the proposed change is good in isolation, as it were, from all the related aspects of community life. It is the extension worker's job to try to tip the scales and he can do this best if he knows the factors that tend to tip the scales against him, so that he can deal with them. He must be as interested in discovering the disadvantages of what he proposes as he is in demonstrating its advantages, and he must be ready to answer people's objections in ways that satisfy them, even if it means modifying in some way his original suggestions. However technically 'practicable' an agency programme may be, it will only become really practicable if acceptable solutions are found for the people's objections to it. Desirably, no innovation should be included in an extension programme until it has first been thoroughly checked for such objections with experienced village workers and with small, sample groups of the people for whom it is intended.

When the agency has decided on its programme it still has the task of training and helping its workers to present it effectively. The first necessity for this is that the workers should themselves wholeheartedly believe in its advantages, a fact that was fully realized by the organizers of the Ghana swollen shoot campaign.

However small a campaign may be it is essential that the teams going into the field not only know what they are talking about, but also have confidence in themselves and the rightness of what they are trying to put across. [24]

This is, indeed, an additional strong reason, if one were needed, for bringing even the lowest grade of field worker into consultation at the planning stage before details of the programme are decided. After all, it is they who work closest to the people and who have the main task of convincing them.

Indeed, field workers can contribute very usefully to both policy and planning. They can suggest what aspects of the proposed programme are likely to be popular and how they can be most effectively presented and explained; what difficulties and objections they anticipate and how they think they can best be dealt with. They can also discuss the kind of aids most useful in helping them to interest and convince the people: for example, the form a wireless broadcast could take and the points it should specially stress; the purpose that could be served by a film, the kind of film, and the kind of audience to whom it should be shown. They may also have ideas about how best to teach some new knowledge or skill required by the programme and of the kind of teaching aid—play, puppets, models, demonstration, or film-strip, that would help them most in teaching it. Failure to lay enough stress even on quite small points may endanger success. In Eastern Nigeria, for instance, propaganda to get farmers to use artificial fertilizer led them to use too much, with the result that their crops withered. How can warnings against mistakes of this sort be most effectively presented? Points such as these must be discussed with the field workers if they are to get confidence in both the programme and the teaching aids with which they are equipped.

People are very many, and field workers are proportionately very few. How then can they most effectively use their time? Should their main approach be to individuals or to groups, and to what kind of individuals or to what kind of groups? If group approaches are preferred, do suitable groups already exist or has the worker to try to form new groups to serve his purpose? For example, in relation to agricultural extension the question should be asked whether any organized groups of farmers already exist, and if not whether there is scope for sponsoring agricultural societies and young farmers' clubs. Again, in relation to an agricultural extension programme, is it worthwhile for the worker to try to contact other groups such as co-operative groups, rural church groups, and even women's groups since in the tropics most women are concerned with food production as well as with cooking? The group approach is important, for as we have seen, individuals more readily act on new ideas accepted by their groups (p. 19), and in general the more groups the worker can interest in a new idea the more readily it will be accepted in the community as a whole.

CHAPTER XII

WORKING WITH GROUPS

In the last chapter we discussed ways of presenting information to people and looked briefly at some of the problems involved. In particular, we saw that purely technical 'solutions' were useless. People's attitudes and feelings must always be taken into account. A solution must be practicable and desirable from the people's point of view.

If the form and content of the agency programme

matter, so too does the situation in which it is presented. Every agency wants to use its workers to good effect. But how can it best use them? Should the main approach be to individuals, to groups, or to the mass, i.e. to the crowd?

While the individual approach to the householder or housewife is often useful and sometimes essential, as a main approach it has two great disadvantages. It is very slow because each field worker has so many people to approach, and it is sometimes ineffective because even if the individual is convinced, often he will not act without the support of his neighbours. This is why so many agencies aim to collect a crowd by using loudspeakers, films, plays and puppet shows, or by organizing exhibitions and demonstrations. In this way they hope to influence more people more effectively.

Such mass approaches are useful for getting people interested, but they are less successful in getting them to act. The agency which aims to influence *behaviour* must usually also contact them in groups.

A group differs from a crowd. People in a crowd may not know one another. In a crowd the only thing they have in common is the same focus for their attention, whether it is a fire, an accident, a football match, a lecture, or a film show.

Because people's attention in a crowd is normally focussed on something external to themselves, and because crowds are often very large, a crowd cannot discuss. Discussion, if any, takes place in the small groups that sometimes form when the crowd breaks up. It is then, and not till then, that group opinion can begin to form.

This factor must be taken into account. Most people

will only act on a new idea when they have had a chance to discuss it with their friends in order to make sure that there are no hidden snags—that what seems good to the agency will really turn out as good *for them.*

Dr. R. G. Ladkin was obviously becoming conscious of this when he wrote an article on 'Health Education in Buganda'. He stressed that propaganda in any subject should be presented to the audience in as many different forms as possible:

To take for instance the all-important subject of hookworm. My experience has indicated that the audience should be shown adult hookworms in a bottle, should be given a formal lecture about the life-cycle of the worm, should see a poster illustrating the way people get hookworms, should see a model of a latrine designed to prevent hookworm, and, if possible, should see a film which animates the worm in its natural surroundings. None of these methods is of any great value by itself, but . . . the combination should be effective.[1]

Of all these methods of conveying information Ladkin stresses most heavily the value of lectures, by which he really means informal talks. 'The lecture', he says, 'is a far more personal method of approach than the showing of a film or poster, and personal contact is essential. . . . You cannot ask questions of a poster, which therefore may be an attempt by Government to mislead you, but a lecturer is there in front of you and if he has stood fast after a barrage of questions, then you are probably convinced.'

Ladkin was quite right in stressing the importance of personal contact in health education, and the same is true of many other kinds of extension work; but in his health campaigns, Ladkin was working with crowds rather than groups, and it is hard for a speaker, however good, to establish close personal contact with people in a crowd. He can stimulate interest, but he cannot easily move people from interest to action. His ideal teaching situation is in the small group.

Why is it important to work with groups? One reason is that the group is well fitted to discuss new ideas, form opinions, and come to decisions about them. The group is smaller than the crowd; its members usually know each other better and meet each other more often than do people in a crowd; and they are more often linked by friendship or by common purpose. All this facilitates discussion and decision-making. And it is group discussion and decision that so often supply the individual with the extra confidence he needs for action. Each individual taking action feels happier because others have agreed to do the same. Moreover, if the decision involves collective action the organized group is better fitted to carry it out.

Ladkin had begun to realize this, especially the importance of stimulating and guiding group discussion. Thus:

A further technique which we intend to try out in the future is to encourage organized discussion groups following the lectures and demonstrations. There are signs that such groups develop spontaneously amongst our audiences and, if they can be organized and directed by African technical staff, they may become an extremely efficient means of cementing the lessons already partially understood.

For this purpose, the worker needs new techniques and additional aids. As we have seen, the film is mainly useful for stimulating interest, but in the group the worker aims also to promote discussion, to give more detailed information, and to teach, if need be, some new skill. He wants the group, not merely to watch and listen, but to think, participate, learn, discuss, and decide. For this purpose, the film-strip and the flannelgraph are far more effective than the film. The film-strip consists of a series of still pictures which are projected on to the screen to a commentary given by the extension worker, and it can be used to give information (e.g. how the disease of tuberculosis is spread); to teach a skill (e.g. how to plant and care for a seedling tree); and to promote discussion and decision making. The advantages of the film-strip are that it is short (usually with from 20–40 pictures); that each picture can be held still as long as desired for questions and discussion; and that the operator can quickly turn back to a previous picture if desired. A still greater advantage is that film-strips can be quickly and cheaply made, so that it is practicable to make them on any, or all, of a large number of detailed, local topics. Flannelgraphs, which have been used for many years for teaching religious subjects, can equally well be used by health and agricultural extension workers to encourage audience participation and discussion. The worker who uses flannelgraphs needs no projector and no source of artificial light.

The main advantage in working with the group rather than the crowd, is that it facilitates discussion, for it has many times been demonstrated by experiment that to encourage people to discuss new information and decide on what to do about it brings far better results than to lecture to them, however good the lecturer may be. Thus during the recent war an experiment was designed to test the relative effectiveness of lecture and discussion methods in changing food habits, for these are ordinarily particularly difficult to change. Six small groups of women were chosen and in every group the same information was introduced, the aim being to get the women to serve such foods as hearts, kidneys, and brains to their families. Three of the groups were given a lecture. The other three groups were given a short talk after which they discussed among themselves the points made by the speaker. Seven days later it was found that while only four of the forty-one women in the three groups who had attended the lecture had served at least one of the recommended meats, no fewer than twenty-three of the forty-four women who had taken part in the discussions had done so.*

That group discussion has this effect has also been amply demonstrated by health and agricultural extension workers in the field. For instance, health workers in the United States have found that young mothers more readily adopt hospital-approved methods of baby care if they are encouraged to discuss and criticize them freely before leaving the maternity ward for home than if they are simply told what they should do.

Group discussion methods have also been tried in some tropical countries, most commonly in the development of co-operatives, but less commonly in health and agricultural extension. One outstandingly successful example of the use of these methods is the Jamaica Agricultural Society.

Early attempts to improve agriculture in Jamaica by means of demonstration plots, lectures, and the distribution of pamphlets had failed, and it was realized that

* For a detailed account of this experiment see Kurt Lewin, 'Forces Behind Food Habits and Methods of Change', *The Problem of Changing Food Habits*, Bulletin of the National Research Council, No. 108, October, 1943.

instructors had to be found whom the people did not regard as agents of the Government or of the big planters. The foundation of the Jamaica Agricultural Society in 1895 was the Jamaican Government's answer to this problem. The Society is an association of farmers, and although it has always been subsidized by the Government it is independent and free to criticize the Government or make representations to it. The Society has its own paid field workers, but its main strength lies in the local and largely self-governing branches which elect sixteen of the twenty-one members of the Society's Board of Management. The functions of the Society as a whole are to supply its members with information by means of its Journal, circulars, leaflets and pamphlets; to help local branches organize local shows and exhibitions of agricultural products and handicrafts; to provide speakers for branch meetings; to procure and distribute seeds, fertilizers, and other supplies and equipment; and to help members to organize themselves for group action in their own interest, either locally or in matters affecting farming interests throughout the whole island.

Until 1950 the Society had its own staff of agricultural instructors, but these were then absorbed into the staff of the Agricultural Department, and the field staff of the Society is now formed of group organizers and project officers. This change recognized that the key to agricultural extension work is the organized group and the discussion which takes place within it. It is the job of the Society to organize and maintain the groups and encourage them to act; the job of the departmental extension workers to bring to the groups the information that the members need.

The Jamaica Agricultural Society now has over 700

branches, and some of the largest branches have a membership of more than 400. It still receives a subsidy from the Government because it has amply proved its value, but it succeeds because it is the farmers' own society, not a government agency. Farmers regularly meet together in their local branches to receive information, discuss it, and form their own opinions about it. If they make a decision, they make it freely by themselves. The real value of the Society to the Government is that it provides the agricultural extension workers with over 700 ready-made and keenly interested audiences of farmers permanently organized for discussion and for criticism or action.

These groups have been useful in a variety of ways not strictly connected with better farming. At one time one of the great threats to the small farmer was praedial larceny—the theft of produce from the farms—and the first attempts to find a remedy failed because the people were unwilling to co-operate with the police in helping to arrest offenders. Then in 1909, fourteen years after the Society was founded, the branches of the Society were empowered to appoint 'authorized persons' from their own locality to arrest anyone they found with produce they could not account for, and it was in this way, we are told, that the nuisance was brought under control. Praedial larceny was checked, as agriculture was improved, by helping the cultivators to take group action in their own interest.*

The principles of group development which governed the growth of the Jamaica Agricultural Society have been applied in extension work of many other kinds.

* For more information about the history, organization, and functions of the Jamaica Agricultural Society see *The Handbook of Jamaica* and also Lord Olivier, *Jamaica; the Blessed Island*, Faber and Faber, 1936, pp. 319–27.

For instance, they underlie the Rural Development Society Movement which was started in Ceylon to stimulate people to undertake village improvement schemes and to become more self-sufficient in the production of food. They have also been applied to extension work with women.

One such example is the Women's Club movement of Uganda. This is designed to meet the social needs of the women in the rural areas and to provide them with opportunities for whatever kind of education they may require.

Like the branches of the Jamaica Agricultural Society these clubs are largely self-governing. They elect their own officers and arrange their own programmes. These may include any of a large variety of activities: cookery, housewifery, dress-making, child care, home nursing, knitting, handicrafts, drama, and music, together with lessons in reading and writing or in elementary English. The clubs undertake practical work in members' homes, organize competitions in home-making and gardening, and arrange social events to which the members invite their husbands. Some clubs organize educational tours, and some have affiliated themselves to the Uganda Council of Women through which they can voice their opinions on matters of general concern to women throughout the Protectorate.

The clubs are serviced by women officers of the Community Development Department. They give advice when they are asked for it, help clubs to find speakers and demonstrators for their programmes, and provide grants towards the cost of the more expensive items of club equipment. They arrange training courses for the clubs' voluntary leaders and help newly formed clubs to organize themselves.[2] There is also a strong Women's Club movement in Kenya.[3]

In work of this kind the agency's main purpose is to make its groups self-governing as quickly as it can. The agency works by serving the common interests on which the groups are based. The members are free to choose what they want to learn, and they learn by doing. Learning and practice go hand in hand.

If this kind of agency work is potentially so rewarding and so effective, why is it so often ignored by extension agencies in the tropics? One reason would seem to be that the staff of some specialist agencies are more interested in what they want to teach than how best they can teach it to the people. This is inefficient extension work and therefore regrettable, but it is also understandable since relatively few technical officers have been as thoroughly trained in the techniques of adult education as in their own specialist field. Indeed, many departmental field officers have had no training in modern methods of extension work at all.

There is a second reason. It is easy to start a group, but easier still for it to fail. This has been demonstrated time and time again in the experience of agencies which work with groups. A group must meet the needs and expectations of its members or it will break up, and if the members of the group lack the knowledge, skill, and resources to do what they want to do, help must be provided from outside.

On the whole, in 'developed' countries, groups need less help than in the rural areas in the tropics, and it is easier to provide what help is needed. For instance, it is easier for the members to elect a literate committee and to find someone who knows how to keep accounts, and there are more educated people near at hand able to give advice and help. Most Women's Institutes in

England can call on a wide variety of speakers, demonstrators, and consultants from within a radius of ten to fifteen miles.[4] In the tropics there are usually many fewer people qualified to help and there are fewer transport facilities. In areas of dense population, e.g., in Uganda, the need is met partly by the staff of the Community Development Department working directly with the groups, and partly by the training courses for the voluntary leaders of the clubs. In areas of sparse population the problem is more difficult, but to some extent it may be solved by the use of broadcasting or by the use of the study-box technique.

One of the most interesting examples of the use of broadcasting in this way is the Canadian National Farm Radio Forum. This project was started in 1941 and is sponsored jointly by the Canadian Association for Adult Education, the Canadian Broadcasting Company and the Canadian Federation of Agriculture.[5]

In essence the Farm Radio Forum is a weekly national broadcast on some topic of interest to farmers and their wives. It is not meant for individuals, but for small discussion groups which meet to listen to the programmes at a member's house. The programme itself may be a discussion of the chosen topic between three or four people or a dramatized presentation, depending on the subject. The aim of the broadcast is to open up the subject for discussion, and additional help is given by means of a discussion 'Guide' which is sent to members before the broadcast. This 'Guide' contains the questions for discussion.

At the meeting the chairman or the secretary will try to get written down the opinion of the group on each of the three discussion questions, and the answers are then sent to the provincial office of the Forum. This office is responsible for preparing a summary of the 'Findings' of all the Forums to be broadcast in the last five minutes of the programme in the following week.

The Farm Forum programmes run from the beginning of November till the end of March—the winter season when there is less work on the farms. Towards the end of this period a questionnaire is sent to each group inviting criticism and comment and asking for suggestions for topics for the following year.

In Canada the Farm Radio Forum has been very successful in stimulating small groups of rather isolated and often not very well-educated people to meet and discuss matters of interest to farmers. The broadcast and the 'Guide' together ease the otherwise difficult task of the unskilled discussion leader and provide a recurrent purpose for the groups to meet, while the weekly broadcast of the 'Findings' helps to make discussion in even the smallest and remotest groups important and significant to their members. The groups also meet a social need. When their discussions are over the members stay on to enjoy themselves with singing, card-playing, or quiet talk with neighbours, and in this way the groups are said to be re-creating community life. They stimulate community rallies and have led to projects ranging from group purchases of garden seeds and the collection of money to have snow cleared from the roads, to the organization of large-scale co-operative enterprises.*

If the Canada Farm Radio Forum suggests one solution to the difficulty of working with groups in sparsely settled areas, the 'Kits' scheme of the Tutorial Class Department of the University of Sydney, New South

---

* For other illustrations of the use of broadcasting to stimulate and service discussion groups see the Antigonish Movement (pp. 67–71) and the San Bernadino Valley Project (pp. 96–7).

Wales, provides another.[6] Faced with the problem of serving groups too scattered and too distant to be reached by its limited staff of tutors, the Department has worked out a scheme by which to reach them. It is based on the assumption that there are many groups in churches and other voluntary organizations who would like to do things together, but who do not attempt any educational activity because they have no one on the spot 'to introduce wider interests and show how these could be developed', and also because they lack sources from which to draw ideas and materials.

The Kits scheme combines the idea of group study with project work. Each Kit consists of a carefully prepared series of from six to nine leaflets, one copy for each member, with a Master Kit for the leader of the group. With the leaflets is sent a box of books and other illustrative material on the project.

Kits began in 1946, and by 1952, 280 groups had already been enrolled for educational projects, yet they occupied the time of only two full-time people. This scheme, suggests its Director, is capable of many other applications in the tropics:

It is possible to visualize a Kits scheme devised to suit the very different needs and circumstances of a South American, West African, or East Asian community. But each case would demand a very thorough examination of the people it was designed to help and the needs it sought to serve. It would require that material be tailored carefully to match the level of literacy, the experience and customs, and the expressed and unexpressed wants of those it was hoped to persuade to use it. For work with literate leaders in backward communities, helping them to advance their own and their people's knowledge and practice in such fields as Health and Hygiene, Agricultural Methods, and a whole range of problems connected with welfare and fundamental education, the Kits scheme would appear to have considerable possibilities.[7]

It is interesting to note here an instance of adult education extension work on somewhat similar lines in the Delhi public library project.[8] The purpose was to get groups of the poorer people to use the library. The first attempts to develop groups on a crafts basis failed, but when it was decided to form groups on the basis of what interested people, success was immediate. Six groups were formed for drama, debating and discussion, literary study, old people, arts and crafts, and music. 'There is no doubt', writes F. M. Gardner, 'that this system of semi-autonomy, with a loose control by the library, stimulated development and created a valuable link between the library and its users.'

In spite of their many differences all these examples of work with groups have something in common. In each case the agency tries to service the group rather than direct it. It aims to find out what people want so that it can teach them what they want to know and help them do what they want to do. In this way it creates confidence and goodwill towards itself and a favourable atmosphere for bringing in new ideas.

This is true whether the agency forms the groups or finds a pre-existing group to work with. In most of the examples described above the agency took the initiative in helping groups to form, but having done so it aimed to make them very largely self-governing. There are several reasons for this. First, the more responsibility group members have and the more they can control their own activities, the more they come to feel that the group is *their* group, not an agency group, and the more meaningful—and therefore educative—the group's activities will tend to be. Secondly, the better a group learns to control its own affairs, the less onerous will be the demands it makes on the agency's group workers and the more they will be able to expand their work with other groups. Thirdly, most agencies value self-government in groups because it helps to develop qualities of leadership and initiative which may help to enrich the life of the community outside the group.

Many development agencies in the tropics have now become interested in working with groups and during recent years have formed new groups of many different kinds. But it is not necessary or even desirable, that they should always try to form new groups of their own. A great deal depends on the purpose of the agency and on the local situation. Some purposes can be achieved by working through existing groups.

Existing groups can be of many kinds: traditional groups based on the indigenous culture; informal work and friendship groups; and other groups such as church groups, thrift and friendly societies, women's clubs, and farmers' clubs, which are the result of past development by voluntary or government agencies.

By developing links with such existing groups the agency avoids certain difficulties and reaps certain advantages. It is less likely to find itself in competition or conflict with other agencies; it works with groups which already have an established place and influence in community life; it appears from the start as a helping and servicing agency, not a directive one; and it is free to work with any groups it can interest in its purpose. Since most changes affect many aspects of community life, the talks the extension worker gives to a women's club, a co-operative group, a progress society, or even a church group may be as valuable as, and often more valuable than, work with one group specially created for the worker's purpose.

Work with indigenous groups is especially important in adult education and social development work. Indigenous groups differ from agency-sponsored groups because they are essentially the people's own groups, formed by themselves in response to their own perception of their social, economic, or educational needs. The kinds of group will vary from place to place according to the local culture and the people's stage of local development. They may include informal village councils, improvement and progress societies, friendly societies, village literacy and project committees, religious societies, tribal or clan societies or clubs, neighbourhood groups, and literary, debating, and political groups. Most of these groups are entirely independent of any external agency. They prize their independence and resist attempts to control or direct them. Many of them are efficiently organized, but many others last only for a short time because their members lack the knowledge, skill, or experience to fulfil the purposes of the group. Whether they succeed or fail all these groups are significant and potentially important. They are significant because they are the fruit of local initiative; important because they can provide scope and opportunity for local leadership to develop.

Such groups provide a rich and rewarding field for educational and social development agencies, but a field, too, which has been hitherto much neglected. This is partly, perhaps, because social and educational agencies assume that they should form their own groups for their own purposes, and partly because successful work with independent groups demands so much skill and patience of the worker, since he is in no sense in control of the situation in which he works.

By contacting these groups and studying their needs, by giving them advice on committee work, programme planning and discussion techniques, and by providing them with printed materials, films and film-strips—i.e. by making available to them the kind of services they normally provide for their own sponsored groups—social development agencies can give many of these indigenous groups a longer and more useful life. And if the activities of these groups are not always those which the agencies would themselves have chosen, they will still be fostering local leadership, aiding local initiative, and winning the goodwill which should enable them to influence and educate more people. And these, after all, constitute the major aims of every social development agency.

Agency purposes and local needs and situations vary so much that it is difficult to frame any fixed criteria for evaluating agency work with groups, but at least one can note certain factors that every agency should take into account. It is in groups that people get social experience and learn social skills. The quality of social life in a community is therefore very largely the product of the experience that people get in groups, and whether it likes it or not every agency working with groups for whatever purpose will inevitably have some effect on social development. This effect may be good or bad. Yet every agency has its own primary purpose which is not necessarily a social development purpose, and the more skilled its workers become in using modern group techniques, the greater becomes the temptation to use them to gain immediate ends. As Treudley writes, 'It is easier . . . to accept scientific findings that can be used in the manipulation of individuals and groups than it is to consider the creation of settings in which such individuals can educate themselves.'[9] To the extent that agencies direct or manipulate their groups to promote their own immediate purposes, to that extent they stifle local initiative and leadership and hamper social growth.

Agencies may also adversely affect social development by accentuating existing divisions between rival village factions. Such factions are common in many rural communities, and they may become important wherever two or more agencies in somewhat similar fields are forming groups in the same community. Each group may then become representative of one faction only and so make existing conflicts more acute. This kind of situation most frequently occurs when the agencies concerned are rival religious missions, but it is a danger which equally confronts agencies of many other kinds. Wherever it occurs its effect is to hamper, not promote, community development.[10]

Both these factors indicate that community agencies should aim to work with many groups in each community rather than with only one; on programmes that are wide and flexible rather than narrow and rigid; and by informal and democratic rather than directive methods. Moreover, it may not be enough to limit agency work to formally established groups. We have noted already (p. 158) that in Jamaica 60 per cent. of the people who attended the Movable School experiment did not belong to any recognized group—to a group, that is, which was recognized by agency workers. Many people, especially the poorer people, avoid such groups. If it is to influence them, the agency must seek out the groups they form among themselves.

Every agency wants directly or indirectly to influence people's behaviour, whether it is to get them to plant a new crop, to bring up their children differently, or to tackle a community project. But it is not enough merely to tell people why they should do any of these things. If the proposed change conflicts with some of their existing values, they will reject it unless they change their values too. Values control conduct.

No agency can force people to change their values. It can only provide situations favourable for such changes to occur. It is at this point that development agencies seem to face a dilemma, for how can they get people freely to accept a new system of values if they are—as in the nature of things they are likely to be—hostile to the new values and loyal to the old?

Kurt Lewin's solution is that agencies should apply certain principles to their work with groups.[11] It is axiomatic, he says, that people cannot be taught who feel that they are at the same time being attacked. It follows that the agency worker should not condemn existing values. He should greatly reduce the gap which normally exists between agency workers and their groups, identify himself as closely as possible with the group, and participate in its activities, rather than seek to control them. His relationship with the members of the group should be such that they feel free to express openly the very sentiments which the worker seeks to dislodge. It is only then that real discussion and learning, in which a change in values may occur, can take place.

For the group to function in this way it must be a real group, that is, a group which members feel belongs to them rather than to the agency. The greater the sense of 'we-feeling' and 'belongingness', the greater the potential value of the group in facilitating value change.

Lewin makes one other point of great importance. 'Methods and procedures', he says, 'which seek to change convictions item by item are of little avail in bringing about the desired change of heart.' Arguments can drive the individual into a corner, but as a rule he will find some way, however illogical, to retain his beliefs. On the whole it is more important for the worker to tackle the basic values which cause resistance to change and to try to influence people from hostility to open-mindedness, and then to friendliness to the ideas and values which he brings.

These principles are endorsed and amplified by Edward Haydon.[12] He distinguishes several possible types of relationship of worker to the group: As *consultant-resource person* the worker shows that he is willing to help the group with advice, contacts, and facilities whenever these are wanted, but he does not try to press his services upon it. If the group finds that he can actually help them and learns to like and respect him as a useful, friendly person he can then begin to influence the group when his advice is sought. In this relationship the worker can serve a number of groups at the same time.

As *sponsor* the worker is in a closer and more time-consuming relationship. He identifies himself more closely with the group, and supports it in some of its activities. As *adviser-coach* the worker comes into the group to give advice or instruction in some knowledge or skill, e.g. football, carpentry, reading and writing, or cookery, that the group wants to learn and he (or she) is competent to teach.

In none of these relationships is the worker a member of the group. He serves it as an outside person, and his influence with it will largely depend on how much it values the services he can give. It was through relationships of these kinds that community development workers in Kenya tried to reintegrate into Kikuyu society numbers of young, educated or semi-educated Kikuyu. Economic and social change had deprived them of their former warrior function without providing them with any worthwhile function in its place, and it was the task of the workers to stimulate them into undertaking new activities. The workers had to adopt a 'spivish' attitude at first to establish a friendly relationship, but they were then able to help them form football teams, to supply them with tools and instruction in carpentry and building, and to stimulate them to use their new skills for the benefit of their communities as well as of themselves.[13]

The worker does not invariably work with groups from the outside. He may become a *member*, accepting the same status as other members and depending solely on his own abilities to win respect and influence. It is an exacting role and one that requires great patience and humility. His outside status may count for nothing, and he will be unable to do well many of the things at which other members of the group excel. He may find his suggestions laughed at, and that he is considered fit only to have odd jobs and menial tasks relegated to him. It may take time and patience to acquire real influence in a group. In spite of its difficulties the member role gives the able worker a position of great *potential* influence, and it is especially valuable for work with anti-social groups, such as urban gangs of possibly delinquent youths. Most of these gangs are not reached by the clubs organized by the social agencies. They either stay outside or, if they come in, try to break them up.

The main hope of influencing them is through the 'detached worker' who goes out to meet and establish relations with the gangs on their own ground, whether he hopes ultimately to draw them into an organized club or not. The qualities, skills, and techniques the worker needs for this difficult task are admirably described by Edward Haydon in the article already mentioned, and by Roy Mitchell in an article called 'Capturing Boys' Gangs'.[14] Both emphasize the need for a patient, flexible, non-directive approach, and Haydon also stresses the need for long-term contact between the worker and the group. But, he concludes sadly, 'the degree of flexibility and long-term contact with autonomous groups which is so important a part of much of what has been said in this paper, is sadly lacking in most of our schools and agencies. Real progress in working with autonomous groups will require the development of more flexible and dynamic programs.'

CHAPTER XIII

SELECTING AND TRAINING THE WORKER

THE many examples of agency work discussed in the preceding chapters show how greatly philosophies, objectives, and methods may vary from one agency to another and from one country to another. Yet in one thing they are all alike, for every agency is in some way or another trying to influence people's behaviour. As we have seen, this is sometimes an exceedingly difficult thing to do, and in the last resort success or failure depends very largely on the skill and enthusiasm of the workers the agency can put into the field. The selection and training of the worker, therefore, is or should be always regarded as a matter of major importance.

In fact, it is only quite recently that most agencies in the tropics have realized just how important training is. Of course, they have always wanted to have technically efficient employees—men and women, that is to say, who know the technical answers to problems of health, food production, and the rest—but they did not worry overmuch about teaching them how best to approach and help the uneducated people among whom they worked. Most workers had to learn this as best they could, some learning from their own mistakes and some, perhaps, never learning at all.

The situation is now different, for many agencies are realizing that the worker is even more important than the programme; that it is his attitude to the people and his skill in working with them that mainly make for success or failure. Such agencies now emphasize method as well as content in their training, and experiment with new techniques in their community work. Some of these experiments have been very useful. They have thrown light, for instance, on the problems involved in developing teamwork between workers of different agencies working in the same area, and between different groups in the same community. They have helped to make clear the uses and limitations of such tools and techniques as films and film-strips, news-sheets, demonstrations, visits and exhibitions, and to emphasize that they must always be adapted as closely as possible to each local situation. They have demonstrated the great value of encouraging really free and frank discussion. Above all, they have proved that the agency's workers must establish good relations with the community's leaders and that these are not necessarily the people who at first sight are most prominent.

The knowledge gained by experiment and practice in the field has been systematized and expanded by much recent research in human relations, leadership, and community organization by social scientists, and particularly by research workers in social anthropology and psychology. Agencies wishing to develop and improve their training schemes now have at their disposal much more knowledge than was available even five years ago.

While knowledge of what is involved in any process of community education is thus rapidly increasing, so also is awareness of the need to use it. This need is most strongly felt in those countries which have embarked on really large-scale schemes of community education, such as India with its Community Projects programme involving many millions of people; Burma, Indonesia, and the Philippines; Jamaica, Trinidad and Puerto Rico in the West Indies; and Ghana with its country-wide scheme for rural education and community improvement. The governments of such countries are now having to recruit many community workers for rural areas, but of the many who offer themselves very few are suitably qualified. As Griffiths points out, ' "underdeveloped" countries contain relatively very few well-educated and well-qualified persons, and still fewer who can be tempted away from their present jobs to work in villages'. Any agency with a really big development programme must therefore largely rely on poorly educated field workers to carry it out, and even these are hard to keep. Conditions in the villages are usually uncomfortable, the work hard, and success slow and uncertain. Even the best workers begin to hanker for the town after a spell in the country.

There is also the difficulty that community development agencies need workers of a particular kind. It is relatively easy, as Griffiths says, to train field workers as moderately efficient agents for enforcing government orders, but this is a costly and inefficient way of using them (see p. 31). By enforcing orders they tend to create resistance and crush initiative. It is also relatively easy to train teams of demonstrators, as in Uganda, to tour the country, explaining and exhorting with the help of films, film-strips, plays, puppet shows, and other visual aids, but unfortunately such teams can stay for only a short time in any one place. Their main value is to stimulate local interest and prepare the ground for the local worker. It is the local worker who has to cope with the real difficulties involved in changing people's attitudes and behaviour, and it is he whose training presents the greatest difficulties.

The local worker needs very high qualities of tact, judgement, restraint, and patience in dealing with his communities, and he needs them too when complaints are made that progress is too slow or results too few. Most underdeveloped countries have not got anything like enough men and women with the skills and aptitudes needed for this kind of work, and getting a good field staff always becomes a crucial problem whenever more is aimed at than the semi-compulsory introduction of certain material changes and reforms.

Governments and agencies are thus facing a dilemma. They need large numbers of men and women of high quality for difficult work under uncomfortable conditions and, be it noted, at comparatively low rates of pay: but all they have available immediately in the required numbers are rather poorly educated and completely untrained men and women. This dilemma can only be resolved by the rapid development of highly effective methods of training for one or more of three groups of community workers: village level workers specially recruited for community development work as, for example, in India, Ghana, and Puerto Rico; subordinate technical staff already employed as rural field workers by central or local government departments as, for example, in Nigeria and Kenya; and local leaders, to whose training particular emphasis has been given in the West Indies.

There are naturally great variations in the kinds of training provided for each of these three categories of workers in different countries, but we can distinguish three general aims which in theory seem to underlie them all. These are (i) to give a *content* of knowledge which the trainee is expected to transmit to the communities in which he works; (ii) to teach *methods* of transmitting this knowledge, encouraging local initiative, and organizing community groups for study and action; and (iii) to raise the worker's *morale* and instil in him a sense of mission for community work.

In most training courses there is more emphasis on content than method, and more on method than morale. Content is nearly always heavily stressed, and in some cases too heavily stressed. Some training courses for village level workers have immense syllabuses filling many closely packed pages with details of the topics the trainees have to study during the few months of their preliminary training. Thus the training programme at one of the first Indian training centres attempted to cover agriculture (general, horticultural, plant protection, and agricultural engineering), forestry, animal husbandry, veterinary work, health and sanitation, co-operation, panchayats, social science, cottage industries, and agricultural extension. Of these, one section only, 'social science', dealt with rural psychology, rural life and culture, village and rural economics, how to find 'felt needs', methods of approach to rural education (individual contacts, group discussion, group action, community meetings, and fixing community projects), techniques of social education (some twenty were separately listed), methods of improving social conditions, adult education (including adult psychology, methods of adult education, recreation, and games), youth activities (scouting, clubs, future farmers of America [!]), literacy classes, village survey, games, finding and training village leaders, and organizing literacy-cum-social centres.[2] Even allowing for the very long working day common in Indian training centres one cannot but wonder how much of this syllabus was actually covered, by what teaching methods, and to what practical effect.

Most training courses also heavily emphasize practical work in which the field worker learns the methods and techniques of applying his knowledge to the actual needs and circumstances of the people. He may get practice in organizing and conducting literacy classes, film shows, exhibitions, visits, and demonstrations. He may handle film and film-strip projectors, and learn to make and use flannelgraphs, puppets, models, and other apparatus. He may learn how to prepare and distribute posters and news-sheets. Some courses even teach elementary library management. Many courses also give instruction and practice in the conduct of informal discussion meetings and in establishing and working with youth groups, community study groups, and action groups. Thus at the Jeanes School, Kabete, the course for community development assistants includes practice in running Young Farmers' Clubs, and for the women practice in starting up Women's Clubs and in conducting their meetings.

All these training activities aim at providing the trainees with the knowledge and practical skills they need to do their work, and naturally they vary considerably from one place to another and with the special purpose of the training. These training activities, too, are relatively easy and straightforward to carry through, always provided that the instructors are competent and the trainees capable of understanding what they are taught. The usual method of training is by lectures or talks followed by questions and discussion, and, where necessary, by plenty of practice: and there is no reason why any properly conducted course, if enough time is available, should not produce men and women reasonably competent to do the work for which they are trained. The real difficulty is of a quite different kind. It is to give the worker a sense of mission. Rural community work is hard, and rural living conditions usually unattractive, and it is extremely important that trainers should try to ensure that those they train will stay on the job for which they are trained, and will develop the patience, tact, and staying power they need for success wherever they have to work in conservative, suspicious, and unco-operative communities.

This is essentially the problem outlined by Griffiths in the article referred to earlier in this chapter, and it is a key problem in the training of every kind of community worker. This is clearly recognized in the 1944 Report on Mass Education in African Society. Voluntary leaders, the report stresses, must be trained to ensure their efficiency and pertinacity. They must be helped to understand the need for development so that they will freely participate and keep on participating in the work of the agencies. As for departmental workers, they must develop a genuine interest in and a personal sense of responsibility for community welfare, a respect for community customs, beliefs, and organization as well as an understanding of adult education as a means of radical community change.[3] Few people, admit the authors of the Report, have all these qualities, but, they say, 'there must be in every Colony a large number from whom a selection can be made with confidence that training and experience will produce the type of teacher required, that is, an individual who is devoted to the service of the community, is capable of studying it and the conditions in which it lives, and of devising teaching methods appropriate to them'.[4]

There is an optimism here about the efficacy of selection and training which has not altogether been borne out by subsequent experience, as we shall see. So much, it would seem, depends on *how* people are selected and *how* they are trained. Unfortunately, most reports of training schemes do not enlighten us much on these two topics, and it is only here and there from the mass of reports that one can pick out anything to indicate that improvement of the morale and attitudes of the worker is recognized as one of the major functions of training.

1. SELECTING AND TRAINING PAID
WORKERS

The careful selection of persons for training is obviously very important, for if the trainees have the desired attitudes to start with, the training problem is made much easier. Yet very few accounts of training enlarge upon the methods by which trainees are selected, apart from stating, as the report (1951) on the Jeanes School, Kabete, does, that important criteria for selection are 'character and ability to lead others'. But how are these qualities actually discovered? Most trainees are selected by interview, but most accounts say very little about the nature of the interview and the methods used in assessing the desired qualities (to quote the Community Projects Draft Handbook for India) 'of personality, initiative, resourcefulness, leadership and spirit of sacrifice and service, simple and intelligent living'. The authors of the Handbook are convinced that selectors should give more weight to these qualities than to the candidate's academic qualifications, and they state the need for new techniques to help selectors to assess them.

This view is also held, and acted on, by the Division of Community Education in Puerto Rico. Here the forty village workers it finally selected for training were chosen from 1,200 candidates, all of whom were interviewed once, 400 interviewed twice, and over 100 interviewed a third time before the final selection of forty was made.

For these interviews the selectors visited the candidates where they lived, and chatted to them unhurriedly, often in the open air under a tree, on a mountain side, or on the bank of a stream. At these informal interviews the selectors were sizing up the candidates. Were they

men of the people and already active in tackling problems within their own communities? Were they pushful
and dogmatic, or broad-minded and adaptable? Did
they get on well with their neighbours? The men finally
selected were of all ages from twenty-eight to fifty-three.
They were mostly teachers and farmers, but there were
also a couple of policemen, a fisherman, a pedlar, a
clerk, a former manager of a large co-operative store,
and so on. All had a rural background.[5]

It is exceptional to find an agency attaching quite so
much importance to the personal qualities of the candidates, and on the whole so little to their academic
qualifications. The more usual view is contained in the
Report of the Mission on Rural Community Organization and Development in the Caribbean Area and
Mexico. This report stresses the need to have workers
'endowed with an understanding, respect and even love
for the people' and chosen from rural families, but it
also stresses the importance of formal education. 'It is
believed that the more extensive formal education is,
the more effective the worker will be.'[6]

All too often the agency which tries to recruit village
level workers of a fairly high standard of formal education runs into difficulties, especially in the more underdeveloped countries, for most of the candidates eligible
for selection will be drifters who for some reason cannot
get or keep the jobs they would like in the towns. Such
persons have no aptitude or interest in working with
rural people, and it is often a waste of time to train
them. While they are working in the village they will be
hankering for the town.

It was to cope with this problem that the Allahabad
Agricultural Institute evolved a very interesting experiment in pre-selection training. It had to select a number

of 'gaon-sathis' (village companions) for training in
extension work. The posts were advertised in the districts in which the gaon-sathis were to work, and application forms were sent to the 800 people who replied.
Then the best eighty were selected on the basis of the
completed forms.

So far so good, but how could the weak candidates
be weeded out? The selectors distrusted interviews, for
they felt that candidates for such jobs are often so ner-
vous, so anxious, and so determined to make a good
impression that an interview could be thoroughly mis-
leading. Instead they invited the eighty candidates to
the Centre for a five-day period of practical testing and
discussion.

Of the eighty invited sixty actually arrived, and six
of these dropped out as soon as they learnt the nature of
the selection course they were expected to undergo. A
few others dropped out during the course itself. The
candidates were formed into small groups and put
through a series of tests. Each was required to learn
a new skill, such as dismantling and reassembling a
plough designed for village use, and then teach it to a
village type of person. They were sent out to visit villages on cycle and on foot. They were taken out in the
evening to find their way as strangers, each man alone
and into a different village where he had to introduce
himself, stay overnight as best he could, and report back
on village conditions in the morning. They did strenuous and dirty work such as compost making or cleaning cattle sheds during the hottest part of the Indian
day. They took part in discussion groups on topics
designed to test their mental attitudes, and they had to
put on an entertainment as a test of their ability to take
part in the lighter side of village life. Six members of

the staff worked with them through this strenuous assignment, and in the end twenty-seven of the original batch were engaged for training.[7]

Selection on these lines is obviously useful, for it reduces the size of the problem to be tackled in training. But what about training itself? How can training strengthen the desired qualities if they are present, or develop them if they are lacking?

Here the main lesson to be learnt from what has so far been done seems to be that the example of the trainers is all-important, i.e. they must themselves establish a relationship with their trainees which exemplifies the attitudes and relationships which they desire the trainees to adopt towards the villagers.

Thus Jackson, writing on Awgu, says:

... In the last analysis the imparting of that idea (of something greater than narrow self-interest) depends on the relationship which exists between the instructor and the pupil. Given that relationship I believe something can be done. The important thing is to try, for without that spirit of public service the best laid plans of community development will go sadly agley.[8]

The 1951 report on the training of Community Development Assistants at the Jeanes School, Kabete, Kenya, is even more specific. To quote,

... It was necessary to ensure that they [the trainees] appreciated the problem and were imbued with the spirit of co-operation and service and learnt how to pass on this knowledge and attitude of mind. ... In every way they demonstrated how we hope their work will be carried on in the districts. The inspiring leadership of Mr. —— largely accounted for their general outlook and behaviour. He never spared himself either when working with the students ... or teaching in class.[9]

Alec Dickson's work in Togoland provides another example. He sees the raising of morale and the development of attitudes as the most important and the most difficult of all training problems, and he relies heavily on the force of his personal example and on the establishment of a friendly and democratic relationship in which all share to the best of their ability responsibility for everything that is done. His training of a team of community development workers was successful in his eyes when, on the eve of the team's departure on trek to Togoland, after saying that responsibility was his if the technique proved a failure, 'the senior African rose and said simply: "There is no question of *your* responsibility; we leave tomorrow as a team—whether *we* succeed or *we* fail." '[10] Dickson believes that in this 'we' lies 'the whole future and adventure of community development work'.

It is always risky to argue from the particular to the general and in this instance Dickson had specially favourable conditions, for he was training a small, specially selected group he was about to lead on a novel and interesting mission. What we have now to consider is how far the same result may be obtained under ordinary training conditions and with the usual type of trainee.

For what Dickson calls 'we-feeling' to develop, the trainees must become strongly identified with the agency's programme and feel personally responsible for its success. This aim is not necessarily achieved by pep talks, lectures, and instructions given by the trainer and based on the authority of the agency for which he works. It is achieved, if it is achieved at all, in a relationship which stimulates very free and open discussion of the agency's aims and methods.

This principle is already well recognized on certain

training courses for voluntary leaders, but it is much less often applied to the training of professional workers, because they are paid employees, and therefore expected to do what they are told. This is a view which ignores the fact that no agency can 'buy' more than routine work. It cannot, for instance, buy enthusiasm and sacrifice. Workers who feel strongly critical of their agency's policies may conform enough to keep their jobs, but they will lack enthusiasm. Men will go on working hard under poor conditions only for ideals they accept as their own and by methods they really believe in. This means that their views must be sought and treated with respect.

This is a hard pill for many agencies to swallow, but what is the alternative? *Kurukshetra*, the monthly journal of Indian Community Projects, deals much more frankly with real problems of this kind than most other journals. Thus the number for June 1953, describes how a group of men training as Chief Social Education Organizers responded to an inquiry from the Chief Administrator. He had asked them what problems they had to face in training, but found them almost entirely concerned with their scales of pay, allowances, transport, and status *vis-à-vis* other government officers. He was disgusted and said so in strong terms. 'We had thought that the Social Education Organizers were being trained to help the villagers. But to them charity seems to begin at home.'[11]

Or were, perhaps, selection and training at fault? Such attitudes are widespread and natural, and they are not confined to India. Indeed, they are only to be expected unless good selection and training methods have been evolved to deal with them. They cannot be dealt with merely by administrators with higher pay and status condemning them. They must be openly recognized and dealt with seriously in free discussion.

The same kind of problem crops up again in *Kurukshetra* in the July issue of the same year, but this time it is the village level workers in training who are criticized. The Administrator admits that their practical knowledge and skills are as good as could be expected after a six-months' course of training, but he is profoundly dissatisfied with their morale and attitudes:

We have discovered that the quality of training imparted to our village level workers leaves a great deal to be desired. What has perturbed us most seriously are the mental attitudes, bearing, and conduct of which we have had evidence from many of them. Some of them acknowledged to be the best from one batch are given to the display of cheap heroics and scarcely veiled contempt and distrust of the efforts and intentions of the administration. . . . It was necessary for me to administer a sharp rebuke at the time.[12]

Again one wonders whether the sharp rebuke was the right answer to this problem, or whether the administration needed to rethink the philosophy and methods on which its training was based.

Too much stress on the formal content of training, and failure to deal with problems of morale and attitude in the trainees, is naturally reflected in what happens later in the field. This can be illustrated by two brief anecdotes, also culled from the pages of *Kurukshetra*. In the first the Administrator meets a village level worker in a backward area and the following dialogue ensues:

'How long have you been here?'
'Four months, Sir.'
'What have you been doing?'
'Collecting data.'

'What about?'

'Felt needs, Sir.'

'What do you mean by felt needs?'

'Mass approach method, Sir.'

'Mass approach method?'

'Yes, psychological approach, Sir.'

The second anecdote concerns another village level worker, very neatly dressed and with a notebook under his arm, found watching a thousand men and women at work on a community project. 'Who are you?' asked the Administrator. 'I am your extension worker, Sir,' he replied. 'What sort of extension work are you engaged in here?' the Administrator inquired. 'I am inspiring the people,' said the worker.

As one reads much of the literature concerned with training, one feels that those who write it are too much concerned with content and method, and too little with problems of attitudes and relationships. Yet selection and training programmes which ignore them are fundamentally wasteful and inefficient, however efficient they may at first sight seem to be. The trainer who aims at securing the full participation of his trainees and at developing their initiative is faced with the same basic problem that faces the worker in the community—he must work *with* rather than *for*, and help rather than direct, and in particular he must allow ample time for the discussion of issues, including personal issues, that really matter to his students. By doing so he may seem to 'waste' some of the time now given to formal instruction in content and method, but by working more flexibly and democratically he achieves important objectives. Learning may be slower, but it will certainly be more real. Moreover, the relationship the trainer establishes with his students will be a living example during training of the kind of relationship the workers should try to establish with the people.

The key to this kind of training is to treat the opinions of the students with real respect, getting them to think constructively for themselves and to draw their own conclusions. Community development is essentially a matter of understanding and working with people, and the trainees will already possess a wealth of relevant but latent knowledge and experience which it is the trainer's job to help them relate to their community work. This he can do by promoting group discussions which should be the core of the course, for these discussions also stimulate interest, modify attitudes, and form opinion. However many lectures and talks are given they should be designed to supplement discussion rather than direct it and control it.

It is at first sight surprising how fertile with sound suggestions and ideas even untrained adults become when they are asked to discuss real problems. Thus when asked to discuss among themselves for half an hour why the New Mexican farmers rejected the heavy-yielding hybrid maize (see pp. 10–11), a group of school teachers from the tropics were able to suggest a dozen good reasons for it, including both the actual cause of failure in New Mexico and all the reasons given by Mandelbaum for the rejection of improved varieties of maize and wheat in India (see pp. 11–12). They were surprised and gratified at their success, which greatly heightened their morale, but it was equally important from the trainer's point of view that these and similar discussions stimulated their interest in people and modified their attitudes towards them. They were less ready to blame failure on people's 'apathy', more conscious of their own need to learn.

But we have to admit that however successful the trainer may be during the period of initial training, the effect is not likely to last unless training of the same kind continues throughout the field worker's service. Indeed, the field supervisor provides the most valuable of all training experiences when he makes frequent opportunities for his field workers to meet with him to reformulate policy, to plan programmes, and to examine methods of work in the light of the field experience already gained. Such conferences, once the supervisor has himself learnt how to work as a member of a team rather than as its director outside and above it, provide the most effective of all learning situations for the supervisor and the field workers alike. They maximize opportunities for discussing real 'on-the-job' problems, they pool the varied experiences and insights of the members for the benefit of all, and they lead to decisions for which every individual member of the group, supervisor and subordinate alike, may feel responsible. Indeed, it is by developing democratic participation in such conferences, more than in any other way, that senior agency administrators may hope to develop in their subordinate workers those qualities of responsibility, initiative, identification with the aims of their agency, pertinacity in the face of difficulties, and real respect for rural people, which are so often lacking in the field worker operating at the lowest, but all-important, grass-roots level in the community.

This is at least partly recognized in a dispatch describing some of the underlying principles of the Jumna Par Punarnirman scheme of the Allahabad Agricultural Institute in which it states that 'the less officer-subordinate pattern with which we can manage the work, the less will our gaon-sathis tend to act in a superior manner towards the villagers':[13] and it is the whole basis of the training and work of the Division of Community Education in Puerto Rico.[14]

Staff conferences and workshops are also a feature of in-service training of community development workers in Ghana. They serve many purposes, but they are especially valuable in helping a team spirit to develop. At these conferences the staff attending are encouraged to evaluate the past policy of the department, including its mistakes, and to help plan future programmes.[15]

In-service training and particularly in-service training of this more democratic kind, is still neglected by many agencies. It has, indeed, the disadvantage that it occasionally takes men away from their work for a day or two, and it also encourages subordinate staff to be constructively critical of agency aims and methods. But if it sends men back to their jobs with raised morale, this is a small price to pay for renewed zeal and more effective work. Also any criticisms that may be made during such conferences are far better out in the open where they can be attended to than left to fester in the minds of the workers with bad effects on their work. Training which neglects the attitudes and morale of the worker neglects the key factors which make for success in all community development work.

Agencies which do not stress in-service training neglect the most rewarding field of all. Training is primarily a matter of learning from experience, and every worker who reflects on his experience and applies its lessons to his future work is engaged in training himself. The essence of organized training is, or should be, to make this (self) training process easier, quicker, and better by helping and stimulating the worker to learn from his own experience and to make accessible to him the experience of others, so that he can learn from that too. But this alone is not enough. For training to succeed, the worker must be interested enough in his job to want to learn; he must be able to see the relevance of the experience presented to him to the conditions under which he works; and he must have opportunities, preferably in the company of his co-workers, of thinking out just what lessons such experience has for him.

Once training is seen in these terms, the need for in-service as well as preliminary training can be clearly seen. The experience provided in preliminary training is never as real as the experience gained by the worker 'on the job'; and the problems presented by the trainer, however real and practical they may be to the people who have experienced them, only become real to the trainees as they encounter them in their work. The worker comes to in-service training with experience and problems of his own. The learning opportunities it presents are therefore more real, and hence more valuable for training purposes, than any that a programme of purely preliminary training can provide.

In all this discussion of the problems of selection and training it has so far been unnecessary to distinguish between general village level workers and the extension workers of the technical departments. The basic problems are the same for both categories of workers. It is equally important that both should understand the people among whom they work, respect them, and establish friendly relations with them. Both types of workers should be equally convinced of the need to work with groups and equally skilled in ways of presenting information, promoting free discussion, and stimulating group decision and action. The main practical difference between them is that the general community worker will more often function as a group organizer, and the technical extension worker more often as a specialist consultant, teacher, and adviser.

One question that is sometimes raised is whether extension training should be provided as a part of the normal professional training of the departmental field worker, or whether it should be organized separately. There can be no general answer to this kind of question as far as pre-service training is concerned, for so much must always depend on local conditions. What can be said with confidence is that frequent opportunities for joint in-service training should be provided for the field workers of the different departments who happen to be working in the same local area. It is a commonplace that co-operation between departments makes for effectiveness in community work, and inter-departmental committees of administrators are often set up to achieve it. But more than this is needed. Real inter-departmental co-operation must involve the actual workers in the field, for in the last resort it depends on how much they see they have in common with each other. Local inter-departmental team work is developed by providing enough opportunities for local field workers to meet at inter-departmental conferences, seminars, workshops, or training days where they can systematically discuss their common needs and desires. 'When they do this, no matter how much they disagree on some things, they agree on some of their common basic needs. It is this agreement that gives them the determination to join hands in meeting these needs.' [16] When Carl Taylor spoke these words he happened to be discussing methods of promoting co-operative action among villagers, but the same principle equally applies to the development of co-operation between community workers. Thus

Mekki Abbas writing of the Um Gerr experiment in the Sudan stresses from personal experience the value that each departmental official gets from discussing the local problems of his own Department with other departmental officials—'We come out with light thrown on our work from various directions and with a gratifying feeling that we are all working for a common purpose.'[17]

Other principles of community work are equally applicable to the training of community workers. Indeed, when it is more generally realized that the principles and methods of community work, i.e. of working effectively with people, apply just as much to community workers in training as they do to ordinary people in the towns and villages, training will be far more generally effective than it is at present in providing skilled and enthusiastic field workers for community development work.

2. TRAINING VOLUNTARY WORKERS

Sooner or later nearly every agency finds that it needs to supplement the day-to-day work of its paid workers with some special arrangements for training voluntary workers. Such training takes different forms and serves different purposes according to the interests of the agency and the needs of the local situation. The training courses may be organized centrally or locally; they may vary in length from a single day to months, or even years; they may be primarily intended to stimulate interest, to teach particular methods and skills, to train existing leaders, or to create new ones. Yet in spite of all these differences every course has the same underlying purpose of ensuring that there are at least a few people in each village willing to co-operate with the agency worker and more able than in the past to help or influence their neighbours.

In general the more directive the agency and the more radical the changes it seeks to introduce, the more it tends to favour central rather than local courses; long courses rather than short ones; and formal rather than informal methods of training.

This is well illustrated by the Rural Improvement School in Sarawak which was established in 1948 as an experiment in educating 'the native peasant in better land use and living standards and in elementary scholarship'.[18] The idea was to collect suitable married couples from the Dayak long-houses and to give them a two-year residential course in methods of farming, black-smithing, and carpentry for the men, and in garment making, cooking, housekeeping, and child care for the women. All were taught elementary hygiene, how to use simple drugs and how to care for the sick. The trainees were provided with rations, lighting oil, a room per family, a little money, and land for raising crops in their free time.

Courses of this kind are expensive, and they are mainly valued as a means of breaking through the hard crust of inertia in strongly conservative communities. By taking even one couple out of each 'reactionary' environment into an agency-controlled environment, and by there teaching and influencing them for a long enough period of time, the agency hopes that they will continue in their new ways *after* training and also begin to influence others.

The results of this policy are often disappointing, for even if the trainees return to their homes convinced that the agency's ways are better than their own they find it hard to convince their neighbours, and only too easy to relapse back into their traditional ways. And the more radical the changes taught by the agency, the more difficulties the trainees will have in introducing them. It was for this reason that the training policy in Papua was to bring in wherever possible more than one couple from each village. 'On their return, each has the moral support of the other in attempts to put new techniques into practice.'[19] It was for this same reason that the Agricultural Department of the Eastern Region, Nigeria, adopted the policy of bringing in for training on its experimental farm at Nkwelle batches of twelve to eighteen farmers all from the same village.

The long, residential training course for village people has such obvious disadvantages that it has never been widely used, but the *short* residential training course is highly valued. By using a training centre to provide many short courses rather than one long one the agency can reach more people; by linking training as closely as possible to the needs and interests of the trainees it hopes to make each course of training more effective; and by choosing for training men and women of local influence and position it hopes through them to influence future thought and action in their communities.

The Jeanes School, Kabete, in Kenya, is one of the largest and most successful residential training centres of this type. It provides short courses of five weeks or less for all kinds of people—for farmers and shopkeepers; for chiefs, community leaders, farmers' club leaders and mission leaders; and for civil servants, teachers, and even librarians, bakers, and athletic teams. In 1954 it provided forty-three courses attended by a total of nearly 800 people.

These courses are all closely related to the interests of

the people who attend them and well designed to give them the knowledge and skills they want, as well as the stimulus which comes from the exchange of ideas and experiences between people with different cultural and tribal backgrounds and attending different courses. The School deservedly enjoys a high reputation throughout East Africa, and one can find many local tributes to the efficacy of its work in Kenya social development literature. A second Jeanes School was opened in Nyanza Province in 1955.

Courses for women are organized separately. The main training centre is at Kabete, but there are subsidiary training centres in many of the districts. Their purpose is to train leaders of women's clubs. Stimulated and helped by the work of the training centres, this women's club movement (*Maendeleo ya Wanawake*) has developed with amazing speed. During 1954 the number of clubs increased from 230 to 508, and membership from just over 10,000 to nearly 37,000.[20]

Training by means of short residential courses is now common in several other African territories. In 1954 Uganda established its own Local Government and Community Development Training Centre at Entebbe on much the same lines as the Jeanes School in Kenya, and in Nigeria the Awgu Centre was established in 1952. Northern Rhodesia has its Area Training Schools, and Ghana a number of Rural Training Centres.

In Ceylon short residential courses of from two to four weeks are held at Provincial Training Centres to teach representatives of the Rural Development Societies and Women's Societies how to run their societies better and how to stimulate greater interest among their members.

The Ghanaian, Northern Rhodesian, and Ceylonese

policy of organizing residential training on a regional or district basis has much to recommend it, even though it sacrifices the advantage of mixing people from widely different areas. District training centres are better fitted than one big centre to deal with local problems, and it is easier for them to organize really short courses for the many people who cannot afford the time to travel to a distant centre. It is presumably for these reasons that a second Jeanes School has been founded in Kenya, and local training centres established for training women club leaders. The training of women is nearly always more popular and more successful if it is organized on a local basis.

The value of local training is also clearly recognized in Uganda, where it is regarded as an important adjunct to the central training organization set up at Entebbe. 'Local training', states a government report, 'is indeed a vital part of the training service in that it is from the results of local courses that selection for central courses can be made and the central staff gains its experience and keeps itself down to earth. Moreover, in local courses agricultural practice can be dealt with in a far more practical way than at any central institution.'[21]

Most local courses have very practical and specific aims, but they are nearly always also intended to broaden the general outlook of the trainees and stimulate them to a more active interest in community development work. For this purpose the residential course has great advantages. Staff and trainees live together, there can be ample opportunities for discussion, and it is mainly through informal discussions that these objectives are reached.

However, such objectives are now considered so important that many centres arrange special courses solely for this purpose. Both at the Jeanes School and at Entebbe there are key courses in citizenship which are primarily intended for local councillors and community leaders, and at Namushakende Area Development School in Northern Rhodesia there have been a series of special enlightenment courses, each lasting one week and mainly consisting of discussions of departmental development policies and local problems.[22]

Nowhere were these objectives more whole-heartedly pursued than under the direction of Alec Dickson at the Man o' War Bay Training Centre in the Cameroons.[23] This Centre drew educated young men, holders of responsible positions, from all over Nigeria, and its four and a half weeks' course aimed specifically at inspiring them to devote themselves on their return to constructive voluntary work in the service of their communities. Each course combined 'two different approaches—a short, concentrated training of the most vigorous and intensive nature, on the lines of a civilian commando course—followed immediately by participation in some scheme of village improvement. . . . The training and field work were geared to extend them to the utmost of their capacity, in the belief that, as in medicine, there was a role for shock therapy.'[24]

These were strenuous courses for trainers and trainees alike, for all 'laboured and strained and strove together . . . in experiences that challenged their manhood', but it was just this, Dickson maintains, that produced a real feeling of common citizenship and of common worthwhile achievement. 'That this reality of feeling could never have been achieved to the same extent by joint discussion groups, by inter-racial meetings, or by common representation on a political legislature, was evident to all.'[25]

It must be emphasized that all the young men were of the clerk-teacher-civil servant type, well educated, but 'reared in a tradition that tends to regard privilege as the right to exact service rather than the obligation to give it'. Thus in a very real sense the Man o' War Bay Training Centre tackled the most difficult of all training problems—the reversal of existing attitudes—and Dickson makes no exaggerated claims to success. He was, however, markedly successful and his methods are worthy of serious study.

Residential training centres are important for the reasons already given, but they can never meet every training need, for it will never be really practicable for enough people to attend them. It is for this reason that many agencies take their training right into the villages themselves, and nowhere has this policy been carried out more thoroughly than in Jamaica and Trinidad.

In many tropical countries the most favoured approach in community development is to the whole community, and in community development training it is to the community's recognized leaders. In Jamaica and Trinidad, however, the main approach is to the small group, and the concept of the leader has been broadened to include anyone, however humble, who has some influence with his neighbours and is willing and able to teach or demonstrate any kind of useful knowledge or skill. From this point of view every group member is a potential leader for whom training opportunities should be provided, and this has greatly influenced the training policies of the agencies. The aim is to provide brief but frequent training opportunities close to people's homes, and to attract people by making the training sessions enjoyable as well as instructive.

The training provided takes many different forms,

and in some villages the Community Council has appointed a special training sub-committee to take responsibility for making local arrangements. *Get-togethers* on a district basis are usually organized several times a year for games, community singing, and talks on village betterment. The main purpose of these meetings is to help people to get to know each other and learn what other communities are trying to do. *Outings* (day educational visits) are arranged for people to see interesting projects in different villages. Groups are invited to send representatives to *Zone Training Days* where they can learn some specific skill of value to the group, such as how to conduct a good meeting, how to prepare minutes, or how to keep accounts. For these Zone Training Days are sometimes substituted *Village Training Days*, and there are also *Village Training Classes* where an expert may meet members of two or three groups to teach them some specific skill.

All these kinds of training are sited at any convenient place—in a school or church or even under a tree—and last only for a few hours. There is no permanent centre for residential training, but residential camps are held every year for the more intensive training of key voluntary workers and leaders, usually at the week-end, though also sometimes for as long as a week or ten days.[26] Some of these camps may be organized as *Workshops*. Training is then centred around some project such as carrying out improvements in one or more peasant homes near the camp, and the trainees themselves do the work. Such workshops both demonstrate to the trainees what can be done and provide them with practice in doing it.[27]

The policies and methods of the many community development agencies, and the local conditions in which they work, differ so greatly that it is only to be expected that their training aims and methods will differ too, but there is also another reason. In many countries community development is a new development, its aims and methods are still at the experimental stage, and its administrators and field workers usually know very little about what is being done in countries other than their own. In one way this is a good thing, for it encourages a very wide diversity of experiment, so that in one way or another nearly every country now has something to teach and something to learn from others. What is now needed is more opportunitity for senior officers responsible for policy and training to make serious comparative studies of the principles, methods, and techniques used in development work. So far, such studies have barely been begun.

CHAPTER XIV

─────────

MAKING COMMUNITIES BETTER

I HAVE not based this book on any arbitrary, *a priori* definition of community development. I have preferred instead to illustrate the different kinds of community development work and to compare and contrast them with one another. The variety is so great that one may well feel that the only thing that community agencies have in common is that all of them are in some way trying to influence people's ideas, attitudes, and behaviour for the better.

In evaluating the examples I have discussed I have tried to see how far the methods the agencies have used have been efficient and consistent with their aims. I have not yet tried to evaluate the aims themselves. But if community development means, as presumably it does, the development of good communities, it is pertinent to ask what in general distinguishes good communities from bad.

I think that the only general answer one can give to this question is that a good community is a place that people like living in because it provides the conditions in which they can lead satisfying lives, and if we accept this it follows that the criterion for success in community development work is that it makes more people more satisfied with living where they do.

This is a simple enough criterion to state, but less simple to apply. If we are to judge community development in terms of people's satisfactions, we have to note that there are satisfactions of many different kinds, that people value some more than others, and that the same satisfaction is valued more by some people than by others. Gardner Murphy points out that some needs are so simple that they cannot provide people with a rich source of recurring satisfactions.[1] Once they have been met, they disappear, and this is a weakness in any community development policy which stresses community projects but which neglects community education. Moreover, while most aims that agencies have for people are good if looked at in isolation from the lives that people lead, we have to recognize that most of them involve some disadvantage for the people as well as the advantage that the agency sees. For the agency's

work to result in real development it must end by raising the *general* level of satisfaction within the community. That is to say, the advantages it brings must
outweigh the demands it makes on people's time and
resources. People must always feel that they are
gaining more than they are losing.

There is another point. Satisfactions are linked to
wants, and wants manifest themselves as tensions—
feelings of discomfort or restlessness—which continue
until the wants are satisfied or abandoned. For most
people today the word 'tension' has rather sinister
implications, for they nearly always meet it in some
unpleasant context of international, political, racial,
or industrial strife. Strictly speaking, however, it is
not tension people are afraid of, but the result of
failing to reduce it: they fear war as the outcome of
international tension, riots as the result of racial tension, and strikes as the result of tension between
employers and workers.

Tensions, however, produce undesirable results only
if people fail to reduce them in more desirable ways. A
tension is a feeling of discomfort, unease, or discontent
caused by some unsatisfied want. This state of feeling
will continue until the want is satisfied, whereupon the
tension is replaced by a state of contentment. For any
individual the process of living is, in this sense, a com-
plicated but also usually an ordered pattern of recurring
tensions regularly reduced, and the tensionless state *per
se* is not desired. If people can reduce their tensions as
they arise they are not worried by them. Indeed, they
may deliberately try to heighten them to increase the
pleasure of reducing them, as, for example, when a
person goes for a long walk to work up a tension—an
appetite for food—so that he may better enjoy a good

meal. Tensions only cause trouble when people see no way of reducing them.[2]

Thus in themselves tensions are neither good nor bad. It is the result that matters. We judge a tension good if it leads to 'development' or 'progress': bad if it ends in some form of disintegration or conflict.

Until recently, most small communities in the tropics provided a satisfying life for the people who lived in them, however poor and backward they might seem by Western standards. This was because life in such communities taught people to expect only what they could reasonably hope to achieve, and when change took place, as it sometimes did, it rarely demanded a quick and major reorganization of a whole way of life. People had time to adjust themselves to it.

The first effect of large-scale development in the tropics has usually been to upset the traditional balance between people's wants and their means of satisfying them, and no one would maintain that most small communities today are as stable and integrated as they were in earlier times. We neither expect it nor, indeed, should we desire it. Community life is less isolated, and the people in each small community are now inescapably members of a larger national society which embraces many small communities: and it is inevitable that they should now seek in this larger society a wider range of satisfactions than their small community alone can offer them. But when this has been said, it is still true that most people in the tropics depend on their own small community for the satisfaction of their major wants. And if under present-day conditions it leaves them with too many wants unsatisfied, the community will begin to disintegrate. People will leave it if they can or, if they remain, will show their frustration in apathy or aggression.

In every culture and in every community people are bound to feel a certain amount of frustration if only because living with other people and needing to consider other people limit the freedom of the individual, leaving him with some tensions unreduced and some wants unsatisfied: and according to Dollard frustration always engenders in the frustrated person some measure of aggressive feeling.[3] Such feeling may show itself in several ways: in open hostility to any person identified as the source of the frustration or, if that is not safe, in aloofness and apathy; or, alternatively, if the source of the frustration is unknown, in a general feeling of irritation which, however illogically, is likely to discharge itself on some person or group on the slightest provocation. It is this general feeling of irritation that Dollard calls 'free-floating aggression'.

Every traditional small community had its own customary means of channelling away free-floating aggression of this kind. In warlike communities it was channelled away in conflict with outside groups: while in peaceful communities it found an outlet in faction rivalry within the community. Indeed, as Murdock notes, conflict or rivalry between opposing factions within the community is one of the main characteristics distinguishing peaceful from warlike communities.[4]

Under these circumstances tension and frustration rarely become disruptive forces in the traditional small community, but the whole picture alters when the community comes under the influence of development sponsored by missionaries, traders, or industrialists, or when it is affected by the development policies of a national government. In any of these forms development imposes change on people, and creates a multitude of tensions far too quickly for people to work out satisfying ways of reducing them. They are continually faced with new demands which create tensions which they do not know how to resolve. Schools and trading stores teach them new wants which they can only satisfy by breaking with tradition and custom, and sometimes only by leaving their homes to work for wages in factories, mines, or on plantations. Even the community worker will sometimes increase the people's sense of frustration by raising their hopes of betterment too high. In the West Indies, writes Hadley, economic resources are so limited that 'West Indian society has never provided the conditions by which the vast mass of the proletariat could possibly hope to achieve through work any rise or improvement of their status', and yet, he says, the community development agencies are teaching the poorer classes of the rural people to value the Western middle-class way of life. This can only intensify the frustrations which already exist, and create for governments the difficult problem of finding constructive channels for the reduction of the tensions they are now creating.[5] Hadley refers only to the West Indies, but the same problem faces every government which educates its people to want higher standards of living than the resources of their country can provide.

What conclusions can we draw from all this about the nature of community development? First, I think, we must note that development always involves change, and that change always involves tension. A contented community is not a developing community. It is a community of people who know what they want and have established ways of getting it. They will only change their behaviour when they learn new wants or have new wants thrust upon them through contact with the outside world. The tensions they then feel provide the motives for change.

All that we can certainly predict when tensions are caused by development is that change of some kind will now occur. People will welcome 'development' and call it good if they can somehow reduce their new tensions and thus widen or deepen the range of satisfactions open to them. They will call it bad if they cannot reduce the new tensions, so that they have to bear with more dissatisfactions than before. Change in the community only equates with development if the new tensions caused by change can satisfactorily be reduced. Failure to reduce such tensions increases people's frustration and dissatisfaction with their community life and may ultimately lead to community disintegration.

There are, in fact, signs that this is just what has been happening in many parts of the tropics. People have become frustrated because they do not know how to adjust themselves to changing conditions well enough to enjoy the satisfactions they have learnt to want. They need help, but the help offered from outside has usually been too small. They show their frustration mainly by apathy towards the agents of the outside world which is the cause of their frustration, and it is perhaps significant in this context how often the words 'apathy' and 'apathetic' have been used by government officers to describe the prevailing attitude of small communities to proposals which might have been expected to arouse their interest and co-operation. There are also more positive symptoms. There is, for instance, the drift of the rural population to the towns, for people are tending to leave their village communities in numbers far greater than the towns can employ. This phenomenon is usually explained by stressing the attractions of town life—the 'giddy-giddies', as people call them in Ghana —but it can also be explained, and often more truly, as an escape from the unsolved tensions of life in the small community.

Another well-known symptom of frustration is aggression. It would be untrue to suggest that there is now more open conflict between small communities than there used to be, for the central governments are usually strong enough to impose the outward forms of peace, but even so there is from time to time quite a surprising amount of open conflict. The Uganda riots of 1949, the Calabar troubles of 1951, and Mau Mau in Kenya, are only three out of a number of recent examples in British-controlled African territories, and similar examples could be quoted from almost every tropical country, free as well as dependent. But possibly still more significant as a symptom of underlying aggression is the very widespread popularity of litigation, which is by no means confined only to the educated classes in the towns. In some areas, for example in Ghana, there is much litigation between communities as well as individuals: and we may suspect that there is some correlation between this growth of litigation and the fact that it is often the only lawful channel people can now openly use to vent their feelings of aggression.

In a very real sense community development is the response of the larger national society to the failure of past 'development' to make ordinary people feel more satisfied with life in their own small community, or even as satisfied as they were before. In one way or another every community development agency is trying to rectify this situation by helping people to reduce some of the tensions that they have so far failed to reduce, or by fitting them better to resolve the new tensions that further change may bring. The community development agency tries to achieve these objects in several ways.

1. *By stimulating people to decide exactly what it is they want, and then helping them to get it.* Many people are dissatisfied generally with life in their community, and remain dissatisfied with it, because they have never pinpointed clearly enough just what they are dissatisfied about. The agency can often help people to decide exactly what it is they want, and then help them to get it by giving them faith in their own ability to help themselves, together with the knowledge and skills they need but do not yet possess. If necessary, it can bring in technical advice and help from outside the community.

Most agencies working in the tropics stress this aspect of community development most of all. Their workers start discussions, feed in ideas, and then try to get the people interested enough to start on one or more community projects (see Chapters VI and VII). If the projects are well chosen they provide the people with two sources of satisfaction: the one, the completed project— the road, the school, the well, or whatever it may be; the other, enjoyment of the process of working together which renews each member's feeling of the significance and value of his group. It is when these *two* forms of satisfaction are present that the project contributes to community development. If the worker rushes the people into a project they do not really want, or if he allows the project to be organized by a minority for its own purposes, the people do not get these satisfactions and the project does not contribute to community development. (For examples of projects of this unsatisfactory kind see pp. 38–40 and pp. 41–3.)

2. *By introducing people to new kinds of satisfactions and ways of realizing them, and by equipping people to make wise choices between alternative satisfactions.* Although project work can be a very valuable form of community development it needs supporting by a long-term programme of community education. Such a programme has many uses. It can help people to crystallize out into specific goals their often vague and uninformed desire for better living; it can help them to choose these goals wisely; and it can show them how to reach them. It need not always result in a group or community project, for it may just as usefully lead to individual or family changes of custom in the care and upbringing of children, the preparation and cooking of foods, housing and sanitation, methods of farming, and ways of spending leisure —changes which may only slowly permeate the whole community. The education which produces such changes is an important part of community development, and sometimes a neglected one.[6]

As changing conditions gradually free people from the restraints of traditional community life and at the same time multiply their wants and opportunities, they have more alternative choices and more scope for making either satisfying or unsatisfying choices: and the community development agency must therefore try to provide people with a background of knowledge, ideas, and experience which will help them to choose wisely, that is to make the most satisfying choice between a number of alternative choices.

3. *By maintaining existing groups or developing new ones to ensure that each individual has opportunities of developing his*

personality and achieving status and significance in his relationships with other people. 'Development' often adversely affects the original purposes and functions of many traditional groups, so that people no longer get the same amount of satisfaction from belonging to them. This makes for the impoverishment of community life. To remedy this the worker must try to help existing groups to adapt their purposes and functions to the new conditions, as well as helping new groups, e.g. co-operatives, farmers' unions, and women's clubs to form and thrive.

Groups are important in meeting both material and social needs, but in practice both agencies and people are more conscious of the need to satisfy *material* wants, for it is in this sphere that the traditional community most noticeably fails. This is dangerous in the long run if it results in the neglect of non-material needs.

What are the non-material needs that people have? Perhaps the greatest is for security in the sense of understanding, or feeling that they understand—and can therefore attempt to control—the forces that affect their lives. In the past people felt that they did understand them. They were supernatural and could to some extent be controlled, so the people believed, by prayer and ritual observances. Today they feel far more helpless, for they now feel threatened not only by the supernatural forces they could influence by prayer, but even more by the remote, impersonal forces and unpredictable pressures of the outside world. They know of no effective way of influencing them, yet it is these forces which are sapping their ability to work effectively together for the common good. People are therefore losing their former basic feeling of security, and to regain it they need to feel that they are gaining control over at least some of the factors that now affect their lives. It is this that makes group development so important, for it is in groups that people can most easily learn, decide, plan, and organize themselves for action in the face of their difficulties. And it is in groups, too, that people can develop the meaningful and satisfying relationships with each other which enhance their sense of personal significance and give them a sense of responsibility for the welfare of others. In the long run it is this kind of development more than any other that reduces frustration and re-creates a satisfying community life.

It is for this reason that skill in working with groups is the basic tool of the community development worker. He values groups primarily because they satisfy material and psychological needs people cannot satisfy in isolation from each other. But he also values them because they provide ideal educational situations for the worker. It is easy in a group to stimulate discussion, and discussion provides a good medium for interesting people in new ideas, knowledge, and skills. But discussion is also useful to the worker in another way, for it helps him to appreciate his aims from the people's point of view, that is, in relation to other claims on their interest, time, and resources, and thus to work more realistically. It is the practical effect of such discussion on the aims of the worker, on the knowledge and attitudes of the people, and on the decisions and action they subsequently take, that constitutes the core of community development, and it is skill in stimulating such discussion that is the hallmark of the good community worker.

I have suggested in this chapter that the aim of the community development worker should be to make the community a more satisfying place to live in, and that the criterion of success should be the increased satisfaction that the people feel. However, this does not mean that in the good community there should be no tension or conflict: neither does it mean that the goodness of a community can be assessed by the number and activity of its groups.

It is tension that makes people act and reduction of tension that produces satisfaction. Thus the community development worker has two functions: the first, to increase tension by heightening people's dissatisfaction with their existing circumstances, so that they become more conscious of their wants; the second, to help people to find ways of reducing the tensions thus aroused. It is only at the second stage that the level of satisfaction is raised, and the Report of the Committee on Malay Education brings this out very clearly when describing the function of the community development worker:

Above all he (the Community Development Officer) is not to be afraid of tensions in the community, or to suppose that he is making a success of his job only when the local people can be pictured as one big happy family. Tensions are the very medium in which his particular art must work. Tensions are evidence of needs, and needs are motives, and motives are the driving power without which social building can neither start nor keep going. In all human action, energies awaiting an outlet break through certain barriers at certain points. The Community Development Officer's business is to identify blocked energies and to help remove the relevant barriers: and to do this in such a way that the achievement of each new popular satisfaction leads to a new series of popular needs (i.e. tensions or motives or dissatisfactions), spaced out along a rising gradient of welfare.[7]

So far so good, but however skilful the worker and however progressive the community, people will inevitably have tensions they cannot reduce and frustrations they cannot avoid, and the community worker must always allow for the existence of aggression originating in this way, and, for lack of any direct outlet, accumulating as free-floating aggression (see p. 220). It is unrealistic to try to suppress it completely, for if it is repressed in one situation it will tend to come out in another, and the worker's aim must therefore be to guide it into channels that will help, or at any rate not seriously harm, community life. This may mean that he will be less worried by community faction because he realizes that it may be performing a necessary social function, or it may mean that he will seize opportunities to stimulate healthy rivalries in recreational activities. For instance, football matches between representative sides may often have much the same therapeutic effect in dispersing aggression as faction or inter-community warfare did in former times, and Murdock even suggests that the British two-party political system has a similar function.[8] The community worker must learn to tolerate aggression and turn it to good account.

In all that has been said so far community development has been represented as a process of increasing people's satisfactions by helping them to satisfy their existing wants, or to learn new wants and ways of satisfying them, or to make more satisfying choices from a widening range of possible alternatives. The effect of this process is to free people from the traditional restraints and limitations of small community life and to give them a new freedom of choice over a widening range of choices. Thus in a very real sense community development means an enlargement of individual freedom in the things that matter most to ordinary people, and it is easy to assume that this is necessarily and intrinsically good, and bound to lead to people living more satisfying lives. But in fact freedom involves responsibility—the responsibility of choice and of accepting the consequences—which many people are unable or unwilling to bear. They find freedom irksome, and want freedom from the responsibilities of freedom even more than freedom itself.[9] Others find deep satisfaction in wielding authority over other people, and seek positions of leadership for that reason.[10] These two kinds of people complement each other, and neither really likes a situation in which everyone takes equal responsibility for decision making, although this is the kind of situation the community development worker is trying to create. Then again, most group and community activities are voluntary, leisure-time activities, and while some people have the leisure to enjoy participation in decision-making, others are too busy, or members of too many groups, to welcome the burden of full democratic responsibility in each of them. All they really want is the right to make their influence felt when they feel that wrong decisions are being made.

These three kinds of people—the power-hungry would-be leader, the passive follower, and the marginal member whose major interests lie elsewhere—are in one way or another responsible for most of the problems and difficulties that confront the group or community worker.

In dealing with these difficulties the worker must try to keep them in perspective and not exaggerate them. He must not expect too much. He is paid to work with groups and he may become even more concerned about the progress of 'his' groups than the members are themselves. His is a full-time interest, but the members are interested only to the degree that they have leisure to take part in group affairs and find satisfaction in doing so, and any one group to which they belong may have to compete for their interest with the satisfactions they get from other groups. The marginal member in one group may have his major interest in another. All the worker can do is provide the opportunities and ideas he thinks may help to make membership of groups more satisfying. The final judgement does not rest with him but with the individuals whom, in the final analysis, all groups exist to serve.

If the worker does succeed in helping people to get more satisfaction from group and community life, he becomes in effect a leader, though not necessarily *the* leader of the group or community, and he acquires the influence of a leader. Both what he does and how he does it acquire significance. To the extent that he consistently shows respect for other people and real interest in their opinions, so he contributes by example to people's appreciation of the practicability and desirability of democratic relationships among themselves. In the long run there is no way in which he can contribute more effectively to group and community development.

REFERENCES

CHAPTER I

1. United Nations, *Report of the Mission on Rural Community Organization and Development in the Caribbean Area and Mexico*, 1953, 45 pp. (The reference is to p. 33.)
2. Batten, T. R., 'The Community and Development', *Corona*, III, 9, pp. 330–1.

CHAPTER II

1. Simpson, C. E. E. B., 'An African Village Undertakes Community Development on Its Own', *Community Development Bulletin*, II, 1, pp. 7–9.

CHAPTER III

1. Nyasaland Government. Domasi Community Development Scheme, *Annual Report for 1951*, Zomba, 24 pp. (The quotation is from p. 11.)
2. *Experiment in Extension: The Gaon Sathi*, Oxford University Press, 1956, pp. 57–62.
3. Wale, F. G., 'Community Education in Puerto Rico', *Oversea Education*, XXV, 2, pp. 46–61.
4. Isales, C. and Wale, F. G., 'The Field Program', in 'Community Change: An Action Program in Puerto Rico', *Journal of Social Issues*, IX, 2, pp. 23–42.
5. Apodaca, A., 'Corn and Custom: Introduction of Hybrid Corn to Spanish American Farmers in New Mexico', in *Human Problems in Technological Change*, (Ed.) E. H. Spicer, Russell Sage Foundation, N.Y., 1952, pp. 35–9.
6. Mandelbaum, D. G., 'Planning and Social Change in India', *Human Organisation*, XII, 3, pp. 4–12. (The quotation is from p. 6.)
7. Driberg, J. H., *At Home with the Savage*, Routledge, 1932, pp. 2–4.
8. Committee on Social Sciences in Relation to Extension Work. *Experience with Human Factors in Agricultural Areas of the World*, United States Department of Agriculture, Washington, 1949, 22 pp. (The quotation is from p. 19.)
9. Sharp, Lauriston, 'Steel Axes for Stone Age Australians', in *Human Problems in Technological Change*, (Ed.) E. H. Spicer, Russell Sage Foundation, N.Y., 1952, pp. 69–90.
10. ibid., p. 89.
11. Paul, Benjamin D., 'Respect for Cultural Differences', *Community Development Bulletin*, IV, 3, pp. 42–7. (The quotation is from p. 46.)
12. ibid., p. 42.

13. Kluckhohn, Clyde, 'Covert Culture and Administrative Problems', *American Anthropologist*, 45, 2, pp. 213–27.

14. Mukerji, M., 'Sexual Delinquency', *Indian Journal of Social Work*, 16, 1.

15. As 8 above, p. 12.

16. Ladkin, R. G., 'Health Education in Buganda', *Community Development Bulletin*, II, 4, pp. 62–9. (The quotation is from pp. 62–3.)

17. Tannous, Afif. I., 'Extension Work among the Arab Fellahin', in *Farmers of the World*, (Ed.) E. S. Brunner, I. T. Sanders, and D. Ensminger, Columbia University Press, N.Y., 1945, pp. 78–101. (The quotation is from p. 87.)

CHAPTER IV

1. Foster, G. M., 'Relationships between Theoretical and Applied Anthropology: A Public Health Program Analysis', *Human Organisation*, XI, 3, pp. 5–16. (The quotation is from p. 13.)

2. Masefield, G. B., 'Reflections of an Agricultural Extension Worker', *Community Development Bulletin*, II, 4, pp. 75–8; III, 1, pp. 8–11; III, 2, pp. 25–7. (The quotation is from II, 4, p. 78.)

3. Batten, T. R., 'A Conference—and Some Reflections', *Community Development Bulletin*, IV, 4, pp. 66–8.

4. Yang, Hsin-Pao, 'Promoting Co-operative Agricultural Service in China', in *Farmers of the World*, (Ed.) Brunner, Sanders, and Ensminger, Columbia University Press, N.Y., 1945, pp. 46–60. (See especially p. 56.)

5. Tannous, Afif. I., 'Extension Work among the Arab Fellahin', in *Farmers of the World*, (Ed.) Brunner, Sanders and Ensminger, Columbia University Press, N.Y., 1945, pp. 78–101. (See especially p. 92.)

6. Mandelbaum, D. G., 'Planning and Social Change in India', *Human Organisation*, XII, 3, pp. 4–12. (The quotation is from p. 11.)

7. Brunner, E. and Smith, C. B., 'Agricultural Extension in the United States', in *Farmers of the World*, (Ed.) Brunner, Sanders and Ensminger, Columbia University Press, N.Y., 1945, pp. 180–92. (See especially p. 186.)

CHAPTER V

1. Batten, T. R., 'Adult Education and Technological Change in Cross-Cultural Situations', *Adult Education*, XXVI, 1, pp. 24–31.

2. Wilson, R., 'Assembly in Madras', *Social Service*, XXVI, 4, pp. 166–9. (The quotation is from p. 168.)

3. Nash, T. A. M., *The Anchau Rural Development and Settlement Scheme*, H.M.S.O., London, 1948.

4. Allen, H. B., *Rural Reconstruction in Action*, Cornell University Press, 1953. (The quotation is from p. 34.)

5. Abbas, Mekki, *Interim Report on the Development of Rural Communities*, Khartoum, 1944, 19 pp.

6. Hardin, C. M., ' "Natural Leaders" and the Administration of Soil Conservation Programs', *Rural Sociology*, XVI, 3, pp. 279–81.

7. Thomson, H. H., 'Peasant Farming Project in the Eastern Province of Northern Rhodesia', *Community Development Bulletin*, II, 3, pp. 48–51.

8. United Nations, *Report of the Mission on Rural Community Organization and Development in the Caribbean Area and Mexico*, 1953, 45 pp.

9. Lord Hailey, *An African Survey*, O.U.P., 1938. (The quotation is from p. 229.)

10. Joint Committee of Community Agencies in co-operation with the Ministry of Public Health, the World Health Organization and Unesco, *Seminar on Health and Human Relations*, Cairo, 1952.

11. Wilson, Fergus, 'A District Team at Work', *Corona*, III, 8, pp. 295–300, and III, 9, pp. 337–9.

12. Ladkin, R. G., 'Health Education in Buganda', *Community Development Bulletin*, II, 4, pp. 62–9.

13. Savage, G. A. R., 'The Use of a Demonstration Team in Community Development', *Community Development Bulletin*, III, 2, pp. 27–30.

14. Wanmali, V. R., 'Villagers' Apathy', *Kurukshetra*, II, 1, pp. 11–12.

15. Hayden, H., *Moturiki: A Pilot Project in Community Development*, O.U.P., 1954.

16. ibid., p. 133.

17. ibid., p. 134.

18. Purseglove, J. W., 'Kigezi Resettlement', *Journal of African Administration*, III, 1, pp. 13–21.

19. Allen, H. B., *Come Over into Macedonia*, Rutgers University Press, 1943.

20. Beers, H. W., 'Survival Capacity of Extension Work in Greek Villages', Applied Sociology Notes, *Rural Sociology*, XV, 3.

CHAPTER VI

1. United Nations, *Report of the Mission on Rural Community Organization and Development in the Caribbean Area and Mexico*, 1953, 45 pp. (The quotation is from p. 33.)

2. Chadwick, E. R., 'Communal Development in Udi Division', *Oversea Education*, 19, 2, pp. 627–44.

3. Batten, T. R., 'Impressions of West African Community Development', *Corona*, VII, 6, pp. 216–19.

4. Ghana, Department of Social Welfare and Community Development, *Advance*, No. 7, July 1955. (The quotation is from p. 5.)

5. Mannin, E., 'Mass Education in Burma', *Community Development Bulletin*, V, 4, pp. 76–8.

6. As 4 above, p. 5.

7. Hardcastle, G. F., 'Area School, Namushakende', *Oversea Education*, 23, 1, pp. 192–3.

8. *The Ford Foundation and Ford Foundation Supported Activities in India*, 1955.

9. Foster, Ellery, 'Planning for Community Development through its People', *Human Organisation*, XII, 2, pp. 5–9.

10. Winiata, M., 'Sociological Principles and Community Development in New Zealand', *Community Development Bulletin*, IV, 3, pp. 47–51. (The quotation is from p. 49.)

11. Committee on Social Sciences in Relation to Extension Work, *Experience with Human Factors in Agricultural Areas of the World*, United States Department of Agriculture, Washington, 1949, 22 pp.

CHAPTER VII

1. Wale, F. G., 'Community Education in Puerto Rico', *Oversea Education*, XXV, 2, pp. 46–61. (The quotation is from p. 58.)

2. Chadwick, E. R., 'Communal Development in Udi Division', *Oversea Education*, XIX, 2, pp. 627–44. (See especially p. 642.)

3. Arsenault, E., 'Social Progress in Eastern Canada: the Antigonish Movement', *Fundamental and Adult Education*, IV, 4, pp. 26–31. (The quotation is from p. 31.)

4. Carney, A. A., 'Education Techniques in the Promotion of Co-operative Groups and Societies in Jamaica', *Fundamental and Adult Education*, IV, 3, pp. 13–16. (The quotation is from p. 16.)

5. Marier, R., 'Social Welfare Work in Jamaica', *Unesco Monograph on Fundamental Education No. VII*, 1953, 166 pp. (See especially p. 95.)

6. Pinnock, A. L., 'Working Together—the All Island Welfare Association', *Community Development Bulletin*, VI, 3, pp. 65–8.

7. As 5 above, p. 159.

8. Hadley, C. V. D., 'Personality Patterns, Social Class and Aggression in the British West Indies', *Human Relations*, II, 4, pp. 349–62.

9. As 5 above, pp. 144–5.

10. 'Unseen Roots of Community Well-being', *Community Service News* (Community Service Inc., Ohio, U.S.A.), IX, 4, pp. 105–7.

11. Rogers, M., 'Leadership and Authority in the Local Community', *Autonomous Groups Bulletin*, VII, 4,–VIII, 1, 57 pp.

CHAPTER VIII

1. Northern Rhodesia, the Department of Welfare and Probation Services, *Report on the Welfare Activities of Statutory Authorities in Northern Rhodesia, 1954*, 16 pp. (The quotation is from p. 9.)

2. Linton, R., 'Youth Clubs', *Social Service*, XXVI, 4, Spring 1953, pp. 176–8. (The quotation is from p. 177.)

3. Allport, G. W., 'Basic Principles in Improving Human Relations', in *Cultural Groups and Human Relations*, Teachers College, Columbia, 1951, pp. 8–28. (The quotation is from p. 27.)

4. Kelly, E. C., *The Workshop Way of Learning*, Harper Bros., 1951, 167 pp.

5. Marier, R., 'Social Welfare Work in Jamaica', *Unesco Monograph on Fundamental Education, No. VII*, 1953, 166 pp. (The quotation is from pp. 53–4.)

6. ibid., p. 61.

7. Batten, T. R., 'Community as "Common Feeling"', *Community Development Bulletin*, III, 2, pp. 21–4.

8. McGairl, J. L., 'Urban Community Development through Adult Education', *Community Development Bulletin*, IV, 4, pp. 71–7. (The quotation is from p. 72.)

9. ibid., p. 73.

10. ibid., p. 76.

11. Rogers, Maria, 'Leadership and Authority in the Local Community', *Autonomous Groups Bulletin*, VII, 4–VIII, 1, 57 pp. (The quotation is from p. 47.)

12. Doddy, H. H., 'An Inquiry into Informal Groupings in a Metropolitan Area', *Autonomous Groups Bulletin*, VI, 4, pp. 5–13. (The quotation is from p. 11.)

13. ibid., p. 13.

14. Johnson, E. I., 'Groups with a Future—In a New Communication System', *Autonomous Groups Bulletin*, IX, 3, pp. 4–15.

15. Mann, P. M., 'The Concept of Neighbourliness', *American Journal of Sociology*, LX, 2, pp. 163–8.

16. ibid., p. 168.

CHAPTER IX

1. Batten, T. R., 'The Status and Function of Teachers in Tribal Communities', *Yearbook of Education, 1953*, pp. 76–95. (The quotation is from pp. 90–91.)

2. Advisory Committee on Education in the Colonies, Colonial No. 103, *Memorandum on the Education of African Communities*, H.M.S.O., London, 1935. (The quotation is from p. 8.)

3. ibid., p. 9.

4. Laya, J. C., *Little Democracies*, Inang Wika Publishing Co., Manila, revised edition 1951, 239 pp. (The quotation is from p. 23.)

5. Ryburn, W. M., *Creative Education*, Longmans, Madras, 1946, 384 pp. (The quotation is from pp. 273–4.)

6. As 1 above, p. 93.

7. Hughes, Lloyd H., 'The Mexican Cultural Mission Programme', *Unesco Monograph on Fundamental Education No. III*, 1950, 77 pp.

8. Capo, C., 'A Family Living Programme in Viani', *Unesco/Ed./ Occ. 19, 1951*, 28 pp. (See especially pp. 11–16.)

9. Maes, E. E., 'The Rural School in Guatemala in relation to Agricultural Extension', in *Educational Approaches to Rural Welfare*, F.A.O., 1949, pp. 1–4.

10. ibid., p. 3.

11. Saiyidain, K. G., 'An Experiment in Social Education: Labour Week in Kashmir Schools', *Fundamental Education Quarterly Bulletin*, II, 3, pp. 3–11.

12. As 4 above, p. 67.

13. As 9 above, p. 3.

14. Orata, Pedro T., 'Basic Survey of Conditions and Needs in Fundamental Education', *Unesco*, 1952. (Mimeo.)

15. Jordan, S., 'Co-operation between Home and School in an American Community', *National Froebel Foundation Bulletin*, No. 79, December 1952, pp. 11–16.

16. Hughes, A. G., *Education and the Democratic Ideal*, Longmans, 1951, 138 pp.

17. Colombain, M., 'Co-operatives and Fundamental Education', *Unesco Monograph on Fundamental Education, No. II*, 1950, 171 pp. (The quotation is from pp. 157–8.)

18. 'School Co-operatives', *Fundamental Education Quarterly Bulletin*, II, 2, pp. 10–16. (The quotation is from p. 11.)

CHAPTER X

1. Laubach, F. C., *Teaching the World to Read*, Friendship Press, New York, 1947, 246 pp. (See especially p. 48.)

2. Indonesia, Ministry of Education, Instruction and Culture, *Mass Education in Indonesia*, n.d., 199 pp.

3. ibid., p. 26.

4. *Unesco World Review*, No. 193, October 1952, pp. 9–11.

5. *World Association for Adult Education*, 'Progress of the Literacy Campaign in Lanao Province, Mindanao, Philippine Islands, 1930–34'. Typescript in Community Development Clearing House, University of London.

6. James, M., 'Promoting Adult Literacy in Jamaica'. *Unpublished MS.* in Community Development Clearing House, University of London.

7. Neijs, K., 'Literacy Teaching for Adults', *South Pacific Technical Paper No. 72*, Noumea, New Caledonia, 1954, 128 pp.

8. Mason, H., 'Progress in Pare', *Corona*, IV, 6, pp. 212–19. (See especially p. 216.)

9. O'Halloran, G., 'Mass Education in Gambia'. *Unpublished MS.* in Community Development Clearing House, University of London.

10. Ghana, Department of Social Welfare and Community Development, *Plan for Mass Literacy and Mass Education*, 1951, 44 pp. (The quotation is from p. 9.)

11. 'Literacy Teachers' Guide', *Unesco Group Training Scheme for Fundamental Education*, Yelwal, Mysore, 1955, 31 pp.

12. Gray, W. S., Preliminary Survey on Methods of Teaching, Reading and Writing, Part II, *Educational Studies and Documents, No. V*, Educational Clearing House, Unesco, 1953, 72 pp. (See especially pp. 35–6.)

13. ibid., p. 33.

14. ibid., p. 35.

15. Sanderson, P., 'Starting a Vernacular Newspaper: Logoiywek', *Community Development Bulletin*, IV, 1, pp. 12–18. (The quotation is from p. 18.)

16. As 8 above, p. 214.

17. Hopkins, R. E., 'Uganda Mobile Bookshop', *Books for Africa*, 21, 2, pp. 24–6.

18. Stewart, M., 'A Book Sales Experiment in Eastern Nigeria', *Books for Africa*, 21, 2, pp. 21–4.

19. Chadwick, E. R., 'Communal Development in Udi Division', *Oversea Education*, XIX, 2, pp. 627–44.

20. As 8 above, p. 213.

(In relation to this chapter generally see also Gray, W. S., 'The Teaching of Reading and Writing', *Unesco Monograph on Fundamental Education, No. X*, 1956, 274 pp.)

CHAPTER XI

1. Entwistle, A. R., 'Literacy by Radio', *Community Development Bulletin*, VI, 4, pp. 86–91.

2. Souza, F. T. de., 'Radio in the Service of Fundamental Education', *Fundamental Education*, II, 2, pp. 17–21.

3. Williams, J. Grenfell, *Radio in Fundamental Education in Undeveloped Areas*, Unesco, Paris, 1950, 152 pp. (The quotation is from p. 111.)

4. ibid., pp. 116–22.

5. ibid., pp. 97–101.

6. Spurr, N. F., 'Try it and See', *Fundamental and Adult Education*, VII, 2, pp. 71–3.

7. Josey, A., 'The Malayan Film Unit at Work', in *Visual Aids in Fundamental Education*, Unesco, Paris, 1952, pp. 109–16.

8. Shirer, W. L. and Pickering, A. K., 'The Potentialities of the Disney Health Films in Mass Education in the Gold Coast', *Fundamental and Adult Education*, VI, 3, pp. 109–20. (The quotation is from p. 117.)

9. Spurr, N. F., 'A Report on the Use of Disney's Hookworm Film in Uganda', *Colonial Cinema*, IX, 2, pp. 28–34.

10. Pickering, A. K., 'Another Walt Disney Experiment', *Colonial Cinema*, XII, 3, pp. 50–53.

11. As 6 above, p. 73.

12. Ogden, J. and J., *These Things We Tried*, University of Virginia, 1947. (See especially p. 261.)

13. Frederick, J. I., 'Adult Teaching with Film in Trinidad, B.W.I.', *Colonial Cinema*, IX, 2, pp. 34–6.

14. As 8 above, p. 117.

15. Ghana, Department of Social Welfare and Community Development, *Advance*, No. 7, July 1955.

16. ibid., p. 2.

17. ibid., p. 8.

18. Campbell, T. M., *The School Comes to the Farmer*, Longmans, 1947, Chapters 5 and 6. (The quotation is from pp. 59–60.)

19. Silvera, H. N., 'Report on a Movable School Technique', *Welfare Reporter*, September 1948, pp. 3–4.

20. Choudri, B. L., 'Come to the Fair', *Community Development Bulletin*, VII, 2, pp. 35–9.

21. Straus, M. A., 'Cultural Factors in the Functioning of Agricultural Extension in Ceylon', *Rural Sociology*, XVIII, 3, pp. 249–56.

22. Foster, G. M., 'Relationships between Theoretical and Applied Anthropology: a Public Health Program Analysis', *Human Organisation*, XI, 3, pp. 5–16. (The quotation is from p. 15.)

23. 'Working with the Village People', *Community Development Bulletin*, VI, 3, p. 59.

24. As 15 above, p. 2.

(In relation to this chapter generally see also *The Health Education Journal*, XIII, 1 (Visual Education Number).)

CHAPTER XII

1. Ladkin, R. G., 'Health Education in Buganda', *Community Development Bulletin*, II, 4, pp. 62–9. (The quotations are from p. 65 and p. 67.)

2. Senkatuka, M. E., 'Women's Clubs in Uganda', *African Women*, I, 2, pp. 45–6. See also P. Hastie, 'Women's Clubs in Uganda', *Community Development Bulletin*, II, 1, pp. 4–6.

3. Kenya, Department of Community Development and Rehabilitation, *Annual Reports for 1953, 1954, 1955*.

4. Jenkins, I., *The History of the Women's Institute Movement*, O.U.P., 1953, 169 pp.

5. Sim, R. A., 'Canada Farm Radio Forum', *Fundamental and Adult Education*, II, 4, pp. 3–11. See also Ruth McKenzie, 'National Farm Radio Forum', in *Adult Education in Canada*, (J. R. Kidd, ed.), Toronto, 1950, pp. 169–78.

6. Wilson, J. L. J., 'Kits', *Community Development Bulletin*, IV, 2, pp. 22–8.

7. ibid., p. 23.

8. Gardner, F. M., 'The Delhi Public Library Project', *Unesco/Ed./Occ./16*, 1952, 26 pp.

9. Treudley, M. B., 'Community Structure and Organisation', *Journal of Educational Sociology*, 19, 9, pp. 576–85. (The quotation is from p. 582.)

10. Batten, T. R., 'The Community and the External Agent', *Corona*, IV, 9, pp. 328–32.

11. Lewin, Kurt, 'Conduct, Knowledge and Acceptance of New Values', in *Resolving Social Conflicts*, Harpers, New York, 1948, pp. 56–68. Reprinted from the *Journal of Social Issues*, (1945), I, pp. 53–63.

12. Haydon, E., 'Methods of Working with Autonomous Groups', *Autonomous Groups Bulletin*, IV, 4, pp. 3–19.

13. Askwith, T., 'The Young Kikuyu', *Corona*, V, 1, pp. 17–20, and V, 2, pp. 59–62.

14. Mitchell, R., 'Capturing Boys' Gangs', *Human Organisation*, X, 2, pp. 26–31.

CHAPTER XIII

1. Griffiths, V. L., 'The Field Worker', in *Approaches to Community Development* (ed. P. Ruopp), W. van Hoeve, Ltd., The Hague, 1953, pp. 218–26.

2. 'Syllabus of Training to be imparted to the Village Level Workers at the Training Centre, Chatterpura (Kotah), Rajasthan'. Typescript in the Community Development Clearing House, University of London.

3. Colonial No. 186, *Mass Education in African Society*, H.M.S.O., London, 1944, 63 pp.

4. ibid., p. 24.

5. Wale, F. G., 'Community Education in Puerto Rico', *Oversea Education*, XXV, 2, pp. 46–61.

6. United Nations, *Report of the Mission on Rural Community Organization and Development in the Caribbean Area and Mexico*, 1953, 45 pp. (The quotations are from pp. 36–7.)

7. *Experiment in Extension: The Gaon Sathi*, Oxford University Press, 1956, 240 pp. (See especially pp. 57–62, 212–24.)

8. Jackson, I. C., 'The Community Development Training Centre, Awgu', *Community Development Bulletin*, V, 4, pp. 81–5. (The quotation is from pp. 84–5.)

9. Kenya, *Annual Report of the Jeanes School, Kabete, 1951*.

10. Dickson, A. G., 'The Concept of a Team', in *Approaches to Community Development* (ed. P. Ruopp), W. van Hoeve, Ltd., The Hague, 1953, pp. 242–4.

11. 'Charity begins at Home! Our Chief Social Education Organisers', *Kurukshetra*, I, 11, p. 9.

12. 'Project Corner', *Kurukshetra*, I, 12, pp. 31–2.

13. Allahabad Extension Department Pilot Project, *Despatch No. 2, August 1952*, Agricultural Institute, Allahabad, U.P.

14. Isales, C. and Wale, F. G., 'The Field Program', in 'Community Change: An Action Program in Puerto Rico', *Journal of Social Issues*, IX, 2, pp. 27–42.

15. Ghana, Department of Social Welfare and Community Development, *Advance*, No. 6, April 1955.

16. Taylor, Carl, 'What should be taught to Trainees with Methods of Group Involvement in Village Programmes', in *Proceedings of the Seminar on Village Agricultural-Industrial Development, Murree*, published by Village AID Administration, Ministry of Economic Affairs, Pakistan, 1954, pp. 71–5. (The quotation is from p. 73.)

17. Abbas, Mekki, 'The Um Gerr Experiment', *Interim Report on the Development of Rural Communities*, Khartoum, 1944.

18. Bewsher, R. A., 'The Rural Improvement School of Sarawak', *Oversea Education*, XXI, 4, pp. 1095–7.

19. McLachlan, B. A., 'A Rural Training Centre in Papua', *Oversea Education*, XXIII, 2, pp. 237–9.

20. Kenya, Community Development Organization, *Annual Reports, 1953 and 1954*.

21. Uganda, Department of Community Development, *Annual Report, 1954*, p. 8.

22. Northern Rhodesia, Commissioner for Native Development, *Annual Report, 1954*, pp. 4–5.

23. Dickson, A. G., 'Training in Citizenship: a Nigerian Experiment', *Fundamental and Adult Education*, VI, 2, pp. 57–63.

24. ibid., p. 58.

25. ibid., p. 62.

26. Burke, E. N., 'Jamaica Welfare', *Community Development Bulletin*, III, 2, pp. 30–6.

27. Francis, S., 'The Workshop Technique', *The Welfare Reporter*, XI, Nos. 6 and 7, pp. 16–18.

CHAPTER XIV

1. Murphy, Gardner, 'Human Potentialities', *Journal of Social Issues*, *Supplement Series No. 7*, 1953.

2. Kluckhohn, C. and Murray, H. A., *Personality in Nature, Society and Culture, Part I.*

3. Dollard, J., *et al.*, *Frustration and Aggression*, Yale University Press, 1939.

4. Murdock, G. P., *Social Structure*, Macmillan, N.Y., 1949.

5. Hadley, C. V. D., 'Personality Patterns, Social Class and Aggression in the British West Indies', *Human Relations*, II, 4, pp. 349–62.

6. Batten, T. R., 'Impressions of West African Community Development', *Corona*, VII, 7, pp. 262–5.

7. *Report on Malay Education*, Kuala Lumpur, 1951.

8. As 4 above.

9. Fromm, Erich, *The Fear of Freedom*, Routledge and Kegan Paul, 1942.

10. Comfort, Alex., *Authority and Delinquency in the Modern State*, Routledge and Kegan Paul, 1950.

SUGGESTIONS FOR FURTHER
READING

MOST of what has been written about community development has appeared in reports or journals. Relatively little has so far appeared in book form. This makes it difficult to select items for a short, introductory list, but I hope that the following suggestions may be helpful to the reader who wants to know what he might read next.

General Reading

While some of the books in this section are not specifically concerned with community development, in one way or another they all contribute to our understanding of the situations and problems with which the worker may have to deal.

Every student of community development needs to have some knowledge, however rudimentary, of human behaviour and human society. One or more of S. Chase, *The Proper Study of Mankind*, R. W. Firth, *Elements of Social Organisation*, and C. Kluckhohn, *Mirror for Man*, are here suggested as introductory reading in these fields.

For the reader wishing to enlarge on this introductory background I strongly recommend J. Dollard, *et al.*, *Frustration and Aggression*, Erich Fromm, *The Fear of Freedom*, Alex Comfort, *Authority and Delinquency in the Modern State*, Bertrand Russell, *Authority and the Individual*, and J. Macmurray, *Conditions of Freedom*. I also recommend G. and M. Wilson, *The Analysis of Social Change*. This short but difficult book provides a good analytical study of the social imbalance caused in an underdeveloped society by the impact of Western civilization.

Two other books should be mentioned here and should on no account be neglected: one is *Human Problems in Technological Change*, (ed.) E. H. Spicer, and the other G. M.

Foster's *Traditional Cultures and the Impact of Technological Change*. With these two should be mentioned the short but very useful mimeographed paper *Experience with Human Factors in Agricultural Areas of the World* published by the U.S. Dept. of Agriculture, and *Underdeveloped Areas*, (ed.) L. W. Shannon. This book contains an excellent collection of articles on rural development and is well worth consulting.

Community development involves understanding and working with groups. My own book, *The Human Factor in Community Work*, should be helpful here. So also should B. and F. Strauss, *New Ways to Better Meetings* and, in spite of its rather strange title, K. D. Benne and B. Muntyan, *Human Relations in Curriculum Change*. E. C. Kelly, *Workshop Way of Learning*, and Kimball Wiles, *Supervision for Better Schools* (again in spite of its title), are both useful studies of methods of working with groups, and H. A. Thelen, *Dynamics of Groups at Work* also contains much useful material.

Community development also involves ability to communicate ideas and information to others. D. K. Berlo, *The Process of Communication*, is not very easy to read but makes some useful points. M. East and E. Dale, *Display for Learning*, is a useful textbook on visual aids, and D. F. Ebright (ed.), *Audio Visual Handbook for India*, is a really excellent practical handbook on how to prepare and use visual and audio-visual materials.

For initial reading in connection with surveys and evaluation I suggest the F.A.O. Agricultural Development Paper No. 52, *Fact-Finding with Rural People* and S. P. Hayes' Unesco Monograph, *Measuring the Results of Development Projects*.

Readers specially interested in training will find my own book, *Training for Community Development*, useful as an initial follow-up to the training problems briefly discussed in Chapter XIII. Similarly, readers with a special interest in making some further study of the part that schools can play in community development might well consult my *School and Community in the Tropics*.

Area Studies

Books. Very few good area studies have so far been written on community development work in the tropics, but S. C. Dube, *India's Changing Villages*, P. du Sautoy, *Community Development in Ghana*, I. C. Jackson, *Advance in Africa*, H. B. Allen, *Come Over into Macedonia*, Roger Marier, *Social Welfare in Jamaica*, and the Allahabad Agricultural Institute's *Experiment in Extension: the Gaon Sathi* are all well worth reading.

Journals, Reports and Occasional Papers

Unfortunately the *Community Development Bulletin* has ceased publication since December 1964, the *Community Development Review* now appears only very occasionally, and Unesco's *International Journal of Adult and Youth Education* has contained many fewer articles of real value to administrators and field workers since it changed its name from *Fundamental and Adult Education*. This leaves among journals specifically devoted to articles on community development only the *International Review of Community Development* published twice a year, and a number of regional journals such as Kurukshetra (India), the *Journal of the Pakistan Academy for Rural Development* (East Pakistan), *Advance* (Ghana), *Leader* (Uganda), and the *South Pacific Commission Bulletin*. There are, of course, many other journals which carry occasional articles of great interest to community development workers. I particularly value *Human Organization* and *Rural Sociology* for this reason.

The Unesco series of *Monographs on Fundamental Education* and the *Occasional Papers in Education* published by the same organization are both valuable sources of information, and the latter can be obtained gratis on application. Most governments now issue annual reports on community development work in their territories. The United Nations has published several area reports of which quite the best so far, in my opinion, is the *Report of the Mission on Rural Community Organization and Development in the Caribbean Area and Mexico*.

INDEX